THE INTERNET FOR DUMMIES®

Quick Reference

2nd Edition

by John R. Levine, Margaret Levine Young, and Arnold Reinhold

IDG
BOOKS
WORLDWIDE

IDG Books Worldwide, Inc.
An International Data Group Company

Foster City, CA ✦ Chicago, IL ✦ Indianapolis, IN ✦ Braintree, MA ✦ Southlake, TX

The Internet For Dummies® Quick Reference, 2nd Edition

Published by
IDG Books Worldwide, Inc.
An International Data Group Company
919 E. Hillsdale Blvd., Suite 400
Foster City, CA 94404

Library of Congress Catalog Card No.: 95-81430

ISBN: 1-56884-977-x

Printed in the United States of America

10 9 8 7 6 5 4 3 2

2A/QR/QU/ZW/IN

Distributed in the United States by IDG Books Worldwide, Inc.

Distributed by Macmillan Canada for Canada; by Computer and Technical Books for the Caribbean Basin; by Contemporanea de Ediciones for Venezuela; by Distribuidora Cuspide for Argentina; by CITEC for Brazil; by Ediciones ZETA S.C.R. Ltda. for Peru; by Editorial Limusa SA for Mexico; by Transworld Publishers Limited in the United Kingdom and Europe; by Al-Maiman Publishers & Distributors for Saudi Arabia; by Simron Pty. Ltd. for South Africa; by IDG Communications (HK) Ltd. for Hong Kong; by Toppan Company Ltd. for Japan; by Addison Wesley Publishing Company for Korea; by Longman Singapore Publishers Ltd. for Singapore, Malaysia, Thailand, and Indonesia; by Unalis Corporation for Taiwan; by WS Computer Publishing Company, Inc. for the Philippines; by WoodsLane Pty. Ltd. for Australia; by WoodsLane Enterprises Ltd. for New Zealand.

For general information on IDG Books Worldwide's books in the U.S., please call our Consumer Customer Service department at 800-762-2974. For reseller information, including discounts and premium sales, please call our Reseller Customer Service department at 800-434-3422.

For information on where to purchase IDG Books Worldwide's books outside the U.S., contact IDG Books Worldwide at 415-655-3021 or fax 415-655-3295.

For information on translations, contact Marc Jeffrey Mikulich, Director, Foreign & Subsidiary Rights, at IDG Books Worldwide, 415-655-3018 or fax 415-655-3295.

For sales inquiries and special prices for bulk quantities, write to the address above or call IDG Books Worldwide at 415-655-3200.

For information on using IDG Books Worldwide's books in the classroom, or ordering examination copies, contact the Education Office at 800-434-2086 or fax 817-251-8174.

For authorization to photocopy items for corporate, personal, or educational use, please contact Copyright Clearance Center, 222 Rosewood Drive, Danvers, MA 01923, or fax 508-750-4470.

 is a trademark under exclusive license to IDG Books Worldwide, Inc., from International Data Group, Inc.

About the Authors

John Levine and Margaret Levine Young were members of a computer club in high school (this was before high school students, or even high schools, *had* computers). They came in contact with Theodor H. Nelson, the author of *Computer Lib* and the inventor of hypertext, who fostered the idea that computers should not be taken seriously. He showed them that everyone can understand and use computers. John would like to thank Ted for letting him hole up on his houseboat during the final editing for this book.

John wrote his first program in 1967 on an IBM 1130 (a computer roughly as powerful as your typical modern digital wristwatch — only more difficult to use). His first exposure to the Internet was while working part-time for Interactive Systems, the first commercial UNIX company, and his system was listed in the earliest map of Usenet (see Part III of this book) published in *Byte* in 1981. He used to spend most of his time writing software, but now he mostly writes books because it's more fun. He wrote *UNIX For Dummies* and *UNIX For Dummies Quick Reference* with Margy and *The Internet For Dummies* with Carol Baroudi. He also teaches some computer courses and publishes and edits an incredibly technoid magazine called *The Journal of C Language Translation* for which all the authors submit their articles by e-mail via the Internet. He has a B.A. and a Ph.D. in computer science from Yale University.

Margy has been using small computers since the 1970s. She graduated from UNIX on a PDP/11 to Apple DOS on an Apple II to MS-DOS and UNIX on a variety of machines. She has done all kinds of jobs that involve explaining to people that computers aren't as mysterious as they might think, including managing the use of PCs at Columbia Pictures, teaching scientists and engineers what computers are good for, and writing computer manuals. She has been president of NYUPC, the New York PC Users Group. Margy has written several computer books, including *Understanding Javelin PLUS* (John also wrote part of it), *The Complete Guide to PC-File, UNIX For Dummies* (with John), and *WordPerfect For Windows For Dummies* (with David C. Kay). She has a degree in computer science from Yale University.

Arnold Reinhold has been programming computers since they had filaments. His first introduction to the hype/so what?/wow! cycle that governs computer industry evolution was the invention of the transistor. He has gotten to do cool stuff in spacecraft guidance, air traffic control, computer-aided design, robotics, and machine vision. Arnold has been on and off the Internet for over ten years. Recent writing includes "Commonsense and Cryptography" in *Internet Secrets* (IDG Books Worldwide, Inc.).

Arnold studied mathematics at CCNY and MIT and management at Harvard. You can check out his home page at `http:// world.std.com/~reinhold/`.

Acknowledgments

The authors would like to thank Barbara Lapinskas for numerous helpful suggestions and sources; Joshua Reinhold for his patience and questions; the many people who created the Internet and filled it with useful information; Max and Grete Reinhold, of blessed memory; Tonia Saxon; Jordan Young; Carol Baroudi; Steve Dyer; Barbara Begonis; Lexington Playcare; and TIAC (The Internet Access Company).

In addition, we have enjoyed and appreciated the feedback we've gotten from readers of *The Internet For Dummies Quick Reference.* If you have comments about this book, be sure to e-mail us at `intqr@dummies.com`.

(The Publisher would like to give special thanks to Patrick J. McGovern, without whom this book would not have been possible.)

Credits

Table of Contents

How to Use This Book

At last — an Internet reference book that includes only the tasks and resources you might conceivably have some interest in! In this book, you will find information about lots of Internet services and how to use them, but we have left out the tons of subjects that will have changed completely by the time this book is printed and that you can easily find for yourself, once you know your way around the Net.

We have also included information about several widely used online services that offer Internet access, including America Online and CompuServe. Topics within each part are generally arranged in alphabetical order. The table of contents, glossary, and the extensive index should also help you find whatever you need.

Finding Things in This Book

This book is divided into sections so that you can find things fast.

Part I, "Getting to Know the Internet," tells you what the Internet is and why it may be the most important technological development of the 20th century.

Part II, "Getting Started," tells you just about everything you need to know to get onto the Internet. A special section is addressed to people who don't have a lot of money to spend.

Part III, "Electronic Mail," explains the basics of e-mail and describes some popular mailing programs. It also has a list of common abbreviations and tips on "Netiquette."

Part IV, "Usenet Newsgroups," explains *Usenet,* a worldwide information system, distributing messages on thousands of different topics every day.

Part V, "Mailing Lists," presents another popular source of information. It guides you in working with the different mailing list servers found on the Internet.

Part VI, "The World Wide Web," gets you started in using the service that has propelled the Internet into the spotlight. It decodes the mysteries of URLs (Internet addresses) and tells you how to use some popular Web browsing programs, including America Online, Lynx, and Netscape Navigator.

Part VII, "Moving Files with FTP," introduces file transfer on the Internet and explains the FTP program in its various guises.

Part VIII, "Finding Resources on the Net," helps you use three popular Internet tools: Archie, Gopher, and WAIS, for finding information stored on the Internet.

Part IX, "Online Communication," shows you how to connect with other computers on the Internet in order to see who is there, send live messages, and even log on, assuming that you have permission.

Part X, "Indispensable Internet Resources," points you to key places to visit on the Web.

Part XI, "Advanced Topics," briefs you on hot subjects like e-mail security, the PGP program, personal home pages, Internet Relay Chat (IRC), and MUDs.

Appendix A, "Internet Connections by Country," lists which kinds of connections are available in each country in the world.

Appendix B, "Usenet Newsgroups," lists some of the more interesting and useful groups in each of the major hierarchies: comp, misc, rec, sci, soc, talk, news, and alt.

There is also a glossary at the end of the book that you can use to look up the terms that you have forgotten or that are just plain baffling to you.

Conventions Used in This Book

When you have to type something, it appears in boldface, like this:

Type **elm**.

When we want you to type something longer, it appears like this:

```
terribly important Internet command
```

Be sure to type it just as it appears. Use the same capitalization we do, because UNIX, the system that most command-oriented Internet providers use, considers the capital and small versions of the same letter to be totally different beasts. Then press the Enter or Return key.

In the text, commands and resource names are shown `in this typeface`.

The Cast of Icons

For each resource or task that we describe — and whenever we provide other important information — we include icons that tell you about what you're reading.

This tip can save you time or keep you from looking like a newcomer on the Internet.

Watch out! Something about this resource or task can make trouble for you.

Who knows why, but this resource or task may not work as you might expect.

This icon points to the speediest way to do something.

A handy cross-reference to other related ...*For Dummies* books that cover this topic in more detail.

Part 1

Getting to Know the Internet

The Internet is just getting started. It will become the primary means of communication in the 21st century. Right now, it is like a new city with magnificent architecture and empty facades, broad boulevards and dirt roads, sumptuous plazas and muddy lots. Swarms of people are already working there, some in carefully planned facilities, others in makeshift shacks. Even though it is only half built, and the architects are continually revising the plans, its diverse neighborhoods are throbbing with energy.

In this part...

✔ **What is the Internet, anyway?**

✔ **What can I do with it?**

✔ **Why should I bother?**

What Is the Internet?

The Internet is a system that lets computers all over the world talk to each other. That's all you really need to know. If you have access to a computer, a modem, and a phone line, chances are you can use "the Net."

The U.S. Department of Defense Advanced Research Projects Agency originally developed the Internet to be a military communication system that could survive a nuclear war. Later, it was funded as a research support system by the National Science Foundation. But that's all ancient history now as support for the Internet comes almost entirely from commercial sources.

Today, an Internet Society tries to make policy and doles out precious Internet address numbers, and an Internet Engineering Task Force sets standards with considerable aplomb. But the real truth is that no one is in charge. It's anarchy at its best and worst.

What's So Great about the Internet?

What makes the Internet great is that it brings together the best qualities of the communication systems that preceded it while improving on their worst features:

+ **Postal mail** (known as *snail-mail* on the Net): Takes at least a day — often a week — to get to its destination, and you need to have envelopes, buy stamps, go to a mailbox, and so on.

+ **The telephone:** The other person has to be there to answer and available to talk.

+ **The fax machine:** Faxes of faxes of faxes become illegible.

+ **The public library:** You have to go there to find information, and half the time the book you want is checked out.

+ **The newspaper:** *They* decide what news you get to see and what spin to put on it (on the other hand, it's hard to line a litter box with a Web page).

Other qualities that make the Internet so compelling to "surf" include the following:

+ Its democratic nature

+ Its capability to let people communicate, even if they are never at their computers at the same time

+ Its basis in text, forcing people to communicate in writing

+ Its relatively low cost to use

♦ Its lack of geographic boundaries

♦ Its capacity to bring together people with similar interests

♦ Its offer of instant gratification

The Internet is also full of contradictions:

♦ It is amazingly fast, yet it often feels agonizingly slow.

♦ It is held together by chewing gum and baling wire, yet it survives man-made and natural disasters when other communication systems fail. (Remember why it was invented?)

♦ It is scandalously vulnerable to hackers, yet it hosts PGP (Pretty Good Privacy, an encryption system), the only really secure means of communication available to the general public. (See Part XI, "Advanced Topics," for information about PGP.)

♦ Its content is often sophomoric, yet powerful corporations and governments fear it and seek to rein it in.

♦ Its day-to-day operation depends on the cooperation of thousands of computers and their human administrators, yet it lacks any central control, operating almost entirely by consensus and social pressure.

No one really knows what the Net will be like in ten years, but one thing is for sure: We won't think of it as a single thing. Different parts of the Net have already developed their own characteristics. No one knows all its intricacies any more than anyone can know all the regions of a large country or all the neighborhoods of a great city.

What Services Does the Internet Provide?

The Internet provides several basic services. They are listed here:

♦ Electronic mail or e-mail (see Part III)

♦ Newsgroups (see Part IV and Appendix B)

♦ Mailing lists (see Part V)

♦ Access to files from remote computers (see Part VII)

♦ The capability to log on to other computers on the Net (see Part IX)

♦ Online database searching (see Part VIII)

♦ Discussions with other people using Internet Relay Chat, or IRC (see Part XI)

♦ Access to the information system of the 21st century, the World Wide Web (see Part VI)

Advanced services under development include the following:

+ Multimedia broadcasts

+ Internet radio

+ Voice conferencing

+ Secure transactions (that is, ways to pay for stuff over the Internet without getting ripped off)

+ Video conferencing

+ Wireless connections

What Can I Do with the Internet?

The list is almost endless. Here are just a few of your options:

+ Send messages to people all over the world at almost no cost

+ Learn the latest developments in thousands of fields of interest

+ Discuss the major and minor issues of the day

+ Search the card catalogs of the greatest libraries in the world

+ Get nearly instant information on almost every conceivable topic

+ Meet new people

+ Find out what your government is up to

+ Shop 'til your fingers drop

+ Find a job

+ Hire someone

+ Tell your political leaders what you think

+ Run for public office

+ Take a class

+ Order a pizza

And lots more.

Most importantly, the Internet is the place to learn more about the Internet. We'll tell you how to get on the Internet in Part II.

Will the Internet Take a Lot of My Time?

Not necessarily. Reading your e-mail and catching up on a favorite mailing list can take just 15 minutes a day. But the Internet can be addictive! There aren't enough hours in a day to keep up with all of it.

People who spend too much time surfing the Net are often told, "Get a life." On the other hand, a recent survey shows that, on a weekly basis, the average American spends 2.6 hours a day watching television and videos. Watching the 'tube ranks third only to sleeping (7.2 hours) and working (3.1 hours).

So, you couch potatoes out there: Turn off the TV and log on! It's happening on the Internet.

Part II

Getting Started

Getting hooked up to the Internet is a lot easier than it used to be, but the process still can be daunting to new users. We'll try to help in this part by telling you what kind of stuff you'll need to go online.

In this part...

- ✓ **Buying a computer for Internet access**
- ✓ **Gearing up the computer you already own**
- ✓ **Getting online without much money**
- ✓ **A quick guide to modems**
- ✓ **Selecting a service provider**

Hooking Up

To use the Internet, you need the following:

+ A computer

+ A modem

+ A telephone line

+ A service provider (the company that connects you to the Internet)

+ Some software

+ Your own copy of this book

Some users, typically at universities and large corporations, are lucky enough to have a *direct connection* to the Internet. These people do not need a modem or phone line, but they may need a network interface card. In almost every organization that provides a direct connection, there is a person who can help you get started. Ask to see the System Administrator. And bring cookies.

Buying a Computer for Internet Access

If you don't already have a computer, you need to borrow or buy one. Computer salespeople will try to sell you the most expensive model they can. Here's what you *really* need to get onto the Internet:

Macintosh vs. Windows

This is a "religious" question. Apple fanatics tout the clean design and ease of use of the Mac software. Microsoft users point out that they are in the majority and claim that Windows 95 makes a PC almost as good as a Mac.

Desktop vs. laptop

Laptops are really cool, but they cost much more for the same performance. Get a desktop unless you plan to travel a lot with your computer.

This year's model vs. last year's model

Computer manufacturers come out with new models every year or so. You can save about $1,000 by buying last year's model. These days, either model is fine for Internet use. If you can afford it, go for the latest: PowerPC in the Mac world or Pentium for Windows. If you are tight, take the bargain. If you're really tight, *see* the section "Getting Online without Much Money."

Lots of the new, snazzy software for the Internet requires a PC that can run Windows or a Mac, but almost any computer can connect to the Internet using a UNIX shell account (described in the section "Local Internet providers," later in this part).

Other stuff

Here's other computer equipment you may want to consider as part of the computer system you use to connect to the Internet.

+ **Hard disk:** Most new desktop machines come with at least 350 megabytes (MB) of hard disk. This size is large enough for Internet use, unless you plan to download a lot of images. In that case, get a 1 gigabyte (GB) hard drive. Hard disks are getting cheaper, so you can wait and upgrade when your disk fills up.

+ **Memory:** Adequate memory (RAM) does more for your computer's performance than processor speed. These days, 8MB is the minimum. Get 16MB of RAM if you can afford it.

+ **Monitor:** The basic color monitor (that is, the screen) that comes with most computers these days will do for Internet use. Step up one level if you feel rich. Anything beyond that level is overkill for the Net.

+ **Multimedia capability:** All Macs come with it; most new Windows machines do, too. Get multimedia capability so you can use the Internet's cool new features, like World Wide Web pages with sound and video clips.

+ **CD-ROM:** You don't really need it for Internet use, but CD-ROM is the Internet's prime competitor for delivery of information. Some things are just better on CD. We recommend it.

+ **Printer:** Almost all modern printers have graphic capability. Any printer will do. You can live without one while you're getting started, but they're handy.

+ **Back-up device:** Hard drives are a lot more reliable these days, but they still crash sometimes. Many are just too big to back up to diskettes. If you are daunted by copying all your files to dozens of diskettes, a cartridge or Iomega ZIP drive (or other removable disk drive) is cheap insurance against data loss. Make sure that you can back up your hard drive in (at most) two cartridges or three platters. Otherwise, you needn't bother.

Gearing Up the Computer You Already Own

While the latest models offer speed and great color graphics, you can use almost any personal computer to get started on the Internet. All you need is a modem and a software package called a *terminal emulator.*

If you own (or can borrow) a 9,600 bps or better modem, use it for now. Otherwise, buy a new 28,800 bps (V.34) modem.

See "Modems," later in this part, for more information. Also, *see* the section "Getting Online without Much Money" if you can't find a terminal emulator.

Should I upgrade my computer?

If your computer is more than two years old, it probably isn't worth upgrading. If you can afford to, buy a new one. Otherwise, save your quarters and wait.

If you do choose to upgrade, just add more hard disk and memory (RAM). Processor upgrades have become more affordable but are often not worth the trouble.

I have a PC; should I upgrade to Windows 95?

Microsoft Windows 95 has powerful features built in for Internet access. But it requires a lot of computer and the installation can go badly.

If you have anything less than a 486DX PC with 8MB of RAM and 100MB of free hard disk space, the answer is no. Wait until you buy a new computer. If you have a 486 or Pentium (and the appropriate RAM and hard disk space), the answer is maybe.

For safety's sake, be sure to opt for the capability to restore Windows 3.1 (in case the installation doesn't work).

See Andy Rathbone's *Windows 95 For Dummies* (IDG Books World-wide, Inc.) for more information about upgrading.

I have a Mac; should I upgrade to System 7.5?

Apple's MacOS System 7.5 also has powerful features built in for Internet access, and installation is a lot less risky than that for Windows 95. But it also takes lots of computer to work well if you install everything. A 68030 Mac with at least 8MB of RAM is the absolute minimum.

Upgrade if you like, but you don't need System 7.5 to surf the Net.

What should I do with my old computer?

Resisting the opportunity to be flippant — we did once see a 286 that had been used for target practice — you have several options for disposing of your old computer when you buy a new one:

+ Let it collect dust in the basement.

+ Give it to your kids.

+ Sell it through the classifieds or want ad magazines.

+ Convert it to a fish tank.

+ Give it to a charitable institution and take a tax deduction.

I prefer the last option. You have enough junk already, your kids will sneer at an obsolete machine, selling is a hassle, and your cats will eat the fish.

There are plenty of worthy places that would be glad to have your old machine:

+ Your local school district or library

+ Your church, mosque, or synagogue

+ A local computer club

+ Organizations that help the disabled, immigrants, underprivileged children, or the unemployed

+ A political cause that you support

+ The East-West Foundation, which collects old PCs (286 or better) and Macs and fixes them up for numerous charities worldwide. (You pay shipping to Boston. Their phone number is 617-542-1234.)

Be sure to get a written receipt that details everything you donated, including software. Tax laws are changing, so get up-to-date advice on how much you can deduct. Check out *Taxes For Dummies,* 1995 Edition (IDG Books Worldwide, Inc.) for more information about tax deductions and other tax-related matters.

Getting Online without Much Money

While you can easily spend several thousand dollars on the computer that you use to access the Internet, you can get by for *much* less money — maybe even none. And you may learn a lot more about computers and the Internet in the process.

Remember: If you want to look only at text, you can use almost *any* personal computer to access the Internet.

Here are some tips for getting started on the cheap side:

+ Check the classifieds and want ad magazines.

+ Go to flea markets.

+ Put up flyers saying that you are looking for a good, cheap, used computer.

+ Let friends and acquaintances know that you are looking for an old computer.

+ If you don't know much about computers, try to find someone who does to help you.

+ Check the local library; many have public Internet access machines.

+ Find a computer club and go to its meetings.

+ Ask for all the software and manuals that the owner of the computer you purchase is willing to part with.

While beggars can't be choosers, here are some suggestions for intelligent scrounging:

+ Old Macs tend to be more usable than old PCs.

+ Try to get a computer with a hard disk, or at least a Mac with a SCSI port so you can add a hard disk later.

+ Try to get at least a 9,600 bps modem. A 2,400 bps modem is usable for text but not for graphics. Anything slower is junk.

+ If you possibly can, plug in the computer and make sure that it works before you take it (even if it's free).

+ Buying anything used is always risky. If you do get stuck, don't get discouraged; just shop a bit smarter the next time.

+ Look for shareware or freeware terminal emulator programs, such as ProComm or Delrina's FreeComm on the PC, ZTerm on the Mac, or Kermit on either.

+ A ton of shareware is available online, but that doesn't help if you are trying to *get* online. One offline source for shareware is

The Boston Computer Society (BCS)
101A First Avenue
Waltham, MA 02154
617-290-5700

Remember: Shareware authors do a lot for personal computing and the Net. Send in your fees!

+ Select an inexpensive local Internet provider. Make sure that it supports the Lynx World Wide Web browser (***see*** "Lynx" in Part VI).

Shareware from reputable suppliers like BCS is generally virus free. Any software you download from the Internet, however, should be checked with a virus checker before you use it for the first time.

+ Microsoft DOS Version 6 and later comes with a virus checker built in.

+ Macintosh users can obtain the free virus checker Disinfectant from BCS and other shareware sources, as well as on the Internet.

+ You must uncompress downloaded files before checking them for viruses. See Part VII for more information about uncompressing downloaded files.

+ Shareware CD-ROMs, available from BCS and others, are an inexpensive, safe, and hassle-free alternative to downloading software from the Internet.

+ It is a good idea to run your virus checker at least once a month and whenever you install software from any source.

Modems

Your modem is the key link between your computer and your Internet provider. You want to get the fastest one on the market. The good news is that you can afford to.

If you are buying a new modem, get a V.34 modem. These units cost less than $250 and run at 28,800 bps, which is as fast as you will ever get on an ordinary phone line. If you are really tight for cash, get a V.32bis modem. It runs slower but is still adequate for Internet use. Don't buy anything less.

In theory, a 28,800 bps modem should run twice as fast as a 14,400 bps unit. In reality, you won't often see a full 100 percent improvement. Here's why:

+ Your phone connection may not be good enough (the modem automatically adjusts to a lower speed).

+ Your service provider may not support 28,800 bps yet.

+ Your service provider, not the modem, may be the bottleneck. This is particularly true during peak usage periods.

+ The Internet itself can get jammed at peak times.

+ Your computer may not be fast enough to keep up.

Modem specs

Modem speeds are specified in two ways:

+ Bits or kilobits per second (bps or kbps). Sometimes people (incorrectly) say *baud* instead of *bits*. Higher is better.

+ The highest International Telecommunications Union (ITU) *V.dot* standard the modem can work with. These names look like V.*nn* where *nn* is a number, sometimes followed by *bis,* which means *and a half* in French. Higher numbers are generally faster, except for V.42, which has nothing to do with speed.

See *Modems For Dummies* (IDG Books Worldwide, Inc.) for more detailed information about selecting a modem.

Unscrupulous vendors sometimes try to confuse you by citing fax speeds or saying V.42bis, hoping that you'll think that's better than V.32bis. If it doesn't say V.34 or V.32bis on the box, don't buy it. Other V.dot numbers may appear also, but it *must* say either V.34 or V.32bis.

If you are buying a used modem, don't pay more than $20 for anything slower than 9,600 bps. Test it before you pay.

Here is a table of modem specification gobbledygook in case you are offered a used one:

ITU V.Dot	Speed	Comment
V.17		The Fax modem standard. Not relevant to Internet use.
V.18	Slow	New standard for talking with TTY devices used by the hearing impaired.
V.21	300 bps	Also Bell 103. Throw it out.
V.22 or V.23	1,200 bps	Also Bell 212A, if you're desperate.
V.22bis	2,400 bps	Okay, if you have no money.
V.24		Also RS-232-D. Says what the serial port plug looks like. Unrelated to modem speed.
V.32	9,600 bps	Decent, if you can get one cheap.
V.32bis	14,400 bps or 14.4 kbps	Last year's model. It's okay to buy one new if you're on a tight budget.
V.34	28,800 bps or 28.8 kbps	The one to get.
V.FC	28,800 bps or 28.8 kbps	An earlier version of V.34. Check with your Internet provider before buying one to make sure that it works with the provider's equipment.

ITU V.Dot	Speed	Comment
V.42 , V.42bis and MNP-5	N/A	Relates to error correction and compression standards. Most new modems support them. Nice to have, but unrelated to modem speed.
V.120	ISDN standard or 57.6 kbps	You need special ISDN phone service.

In or out? Modem types

There are two types of modems: *external* modems, which are a separate box that sits on your desk, and *internal* modems, which mount inside your computer. The main difference between external modems for PCs and Macs is the cable and the software. Internal modems work only with the model of computer they are made for.

We like external modems because you can see what's going on by looking at the lights. (*See* "What do the lights on my modem mean?" later in this section.)

When buying a modem, always buy one that's made for your computer.

Other modem jargon

 ✦ **Baud rate:** How fast your modem can send data

 ✦ **CCITT:** The old name for the ITU-T international committee that set worldwide communication specifications

 ✦ **DB-25:** The style of data plug on most modems and serial ports, shaped like a 2-inch high, skinny letter *D* with 25 pins (Macs use a smaller, round plug)

 ✦ **Group 3:** The type of fax everyone uses these days

 ✦ **Initialization string:** The message that your communication software sends to your modem to get it set up right. Your modem's manual should tell you what to use. If all else fails, use ATZ.

 ✦ **ISDN:** Integrated Services Digital Network, a faster, digital phone service that operates at speeds of up to 128 kilobits per second

 ✦ **Modem:** Short for *modulator/demodulator;* the little box that connects your computer to a phone line

 ✦ **Parity:** Just say **none**

 ✦ **PCMCIA or PC card modems:** Little units that look like fat credit cards; usable in many laptops

 ✦ **Serial port:** The place on the back of your computer into which you plug your modem

- **Stop bits:** Just say **1**
- **XON/XOFF:** One way for your computer to say "wait a bit" when data is coming in too fast; the other way is usually called *hardware*
- **XModem:** A protocol for sending files between computers; second choice after ZModem
- **ZModem:** A protocol for sending files between computers; generally the best one to use

What do the lights on my modem mean?

TIP

Here is a quick guide to modem lights, followed by a table of the most common ones.

- If a bunch of lights are on and some are blinking or dim, your modem is hard at work and all is well.
- If a couple of lights are on steadily, you haven't logged in yet or you've lost your connection.
- If no lights are on, the switch in the back of the modem is off, the modem's power module isn't plugged in, or the modem is broken.

The following table lists some common modem lights and what they mean. Your modem's manual should include a complete list.

Label	*Name*	*Meaning*
AA	Auto-answer	The modem may answer the phone.
CD	Carrier Detect	The modem is connected to another computer.
DC	Data Compression	Your modem and the modem to which it's connecting have agreed to use compression.
EC	Error Correction	Your modem and the modem to which it's connecting have agreed to use error correction.
HS	High speed	Your modem is ready to go at at least 4,800 bps.
MR	Modem Ready	The power is on.
OH	Off Hook	The modem has "picked up the phone."
RD	Receive data	Blinks when the modem is receiving data.
SD	Send data	Blinks when the modem is talking to your computer.
TR	Terminal Ready	Your computer is ready for data.
TM	Test mode	Flashes when you first turn on your modem. Later, it means that your modem sees an error.
V.*nn*		Your modem is using the V.*nn* protocol

Other modem tips

+ If someone picks up an extension phone while you are logged in, it usually breaks your connection.

+ If you have call waiting, put ***70** in front of the number of your Internet service provider in your communication software to turn off call waiting while your modem is in use.

+ If your modem dies, buy a new one. They are usually not worth repairing.

+ While there are a zillion brands of modems, internally they all use one of a few sets of chips from one of a handful of suppliers. The chip set determines how a modem works.

Telephone line tips

Your ordinary phone line is all you need to connect to the Internet. If you end up tying up the phone a lot, you may want to get a second line. Here are some other tips:

+ If your phone company gives you a choice of local service options, pick one that lets you call your Internet provider without per-minute charges.

+ You need a modular phone jack to plug in your modem. If you don't have one, Radio Shack stores carry a wide line of adapters and wiring stuff.

+ If you do get a second line, don't add extensions and don't get call waiting.

+ Business service costs a lot more than residential service.

ISDN

V.34 (28.8 kbps) modems have just about reached the theoretical speed limit for ordinary (analog) phone lines. To go any faster, you need to get a different type of link to your Internet provider. ISDN, which stands for *Integrated Services Digital Network*, is a hot contender. The ISDN link can operate at five times the speed of V.34 and should work with your existing phone wiring.

In a few years, everyone may be using it, but right now, it's too expensive and complicated for most people. If you want to be an ISDN pioneer and really impress your friends, get a copy of *ISDN For Dummies* (IDG Books Worldwide, Inc.).

Selecting an Internet Provider

Once you have a computer and a modem, you need a service provider. The provider is your gateway to the Net. Types of service providers are described in the following sections as commercial online services, local providers, and direct connection.

Commercial online services

This type of provider tries to offer much more than basic Internet access in order to get you to use its services. Needless to say, these providers charge more as a result. Reasons for picking a commercial online service include the following:

◆ User-friendly interface

◆ Added services that are local to that provider

◆ Capability to log in from any major city just by making a local phone call

◆ Better security

◆ Longevity

◆ Lots of user support

The commercial online services provide a great deal of user support, but when something new comes along, months (or even years) may pass before they can offer it.

If you call, the major commercial providers will send you a starter kit with the software you need, and usually some type of promotional offer. A listing of the top online services follows:

Service	Phone Number (s)
America Online (AOL)	800-827-6364; 703-448-8700
CompuServe	800-848-8990; 614-529-1340
Delphi	800-695-4005; 617-491-3393
eWorld (Macintosh only)	800-775-4556; 408-996-1010
GEnie	800-638-9636; 301-340-5216; TDD 800-238-9172
The Microsoft Network (MSN)	Software bundled with Windows 95; 800-386-5550
Prodigy	800-776-3449, 914-448-8000

America Online has launched a new subsidiary called Global Network Navigator (GNN) that provides services similar to the local providers, but with AOL's network of phone connections. You can contact GNN at 800-819-6112.

Local Internet providers

Local Internet providers come in two flavors:

✦ **SLIP/PPP dial-up:** Your computer is connected directly to the Internet. You provide the connection software on your end (although some local providers help you with this). You can use cool graphics programs like Eudora, FreeAgent, and Netscape.

✦ **Terminal or shell dial-up:** Your computer acts like a terminal to a yucky, old-fashioned UNIX time-sharing service. You have to learn UNIX commands, and you can't use neat new graphics programs unless you use TIA (see the following paragraph).

Programs like TIA and SLIRP let terminal dial-up providers offer service similar to SLIP and PPP providers. These programs make the distinction between the two types of local providers less important. To find out about TIA, send a blank e-mail message to

```
tia-info@marketplace.com
```

In case you are curious, SLIP stands for *Serial Line Internet Protocol* and PPP stands for *Point to Point Protocol.* These protocols do pretty much the same thing. If you have a choice, PPP is slightly preferable. For more information about SLIP and PPP, see *The Internet For Dummies,* 3rd Edition (IDG Books Worldwide, Inc.).

Reasons to go local include the following:

✦ Lower cost; many providers offer a flat monthly rate

✦ Higher speeds

✦ Choice of access tools (Mosaic, Netscape, Eudora, and so on)

✦ Capability to use the latest Internet services as soon as they hit the Net

✦ Less censorship

✦ Higher status in the Internet pecking order

To find a local Internet provider, ask around or check the business pages in your local newspaper. Consider the following things when picking one:

✦ Flat fee versus hourly charge

✦ System availability during peak periods

✦ Availability of new services such as home pages

✦ Modem speeds

✦ Reciprocal arrangements with providers in other locations

✦ Appropriate support (If you are a Macintosh user, make sure that your provider offers whole-hearted support for Macintosh Internet applications.)

It is not unreasonable to try several services before picking the one you like best. But remember, once you start giving out your e-mail address, you may find it harder to switch services.

Direct connection

If the computer networks at your organization are connected to the Internet, your computer is already on the Net, and you can use Internet facilities directly. Talk to your network administrator to find out what you need to do.

See Chapter 2 of *The Internet For Dummies,* 3rd Edition for more information.

Protocols Used on the Internet

Protocols are the agreed-upon rules that computers rely on to talk among themselves. The following table lists some of the more important Internet protocols:

Protocol	What It Is
IP (Internet Protocol)	The underlying protocol used to pass data from one Internet host to another
TCP (Transfer Control Protocol)	Used for applications that need a continuing connection between two computers, such as remote login; always used in connection with IP; often known as TCP/IP
UDP (User Datagram Protocol)	Parallel to TCP, used for applications that send one-shot messages to each other
SMTP (Simple Mail Transfer Protocol)	Misnamed protocol used to transfer e-mail from one host to another
ARP (Address Resolution Protocol)	Specialized protocol used to identify hosts on an Ethernet local network
ICMP (Internet Control Message Protocol)	Used to pass control and error messages
FTP (File Transfer Protocol)	Used by the FTP program to transfer files from one host to another
HTTP (HyperText Transfer Protocol)	Used to pass information in the World Wide Web

Protocol	What It Is
HTTPS (Secure HyperText Transfer Protocol)	Uses SSL to pass information in the World Wide Web securely
SSL (Secure Socket Layer)	A technology that lets one computer verify another's identity and allows secure connections

Part III

Electronic Mail

Electronic mail, or *e-mail,* is without a doubt the most widely used Internet service. Internet mail is connected to most other mail systems. *See* "Mailing to Non-Internet Systems," in this part.

To use e-mail, you need a mail program, or *mailer. See* "Mailers," in this part.

In this part...

- ✔ **Abbreviations**
- ✔ **Addresses**
- ✔ **Caveats**
- ✔ **Etiquette**
- ✔ **FAX**
- ✔ **Finding e-mail addresses**
- ✔ **Headers**
- ✔ **Mailers, including AOL, CompuServe, elm, Pine, and Prodigy**
- ✔ **Notification of arriving mail**
- ✔ **Postmaster**
- ✔ **Sending mail to other online services**
- ✔ **Smileys and emoticons**
- ✔ **X.400 and X.500**

Abbreviations

EUOA! (E-mail users often abbreviate.) Here are some of the most widely used abbreviations:

Abbreviation	What It Means
AFAIK	As Far As I Know
AKA	Also Known As
BTW	By The Way
FAQ	Frequently Asked Question (**see** "Newsgroups," in Part IV)
FYI	For Your Information
IMHO	In My Humble Opinion
IMNSHO	In My Not So Humble Opinion
NRN	No Response Necessary
LOL	Laughing Out Loud
RSN	Real Soon Now (Not!)
ROTFL	Rolling On The Floor, Laughing
RTFM	Read The *@$% Manual (you should have looked it up yourself)
TIA	Thanks In Advance
TLA	Three-Letter Acronym
WRT	With Respect To
WYSIWYG	What You See Is What You Get
YMMV	Your Mileage May Vary

For lots more abbreviations and acronyms, check out *Babel: A Glossary Of Computer Oriented Abbreviations And Acronyms* at this URL (see Part VI for what to do with a URL):

```
URL: http://www.access.digex.net/~ikind/babel95c.html
```

See also "Smileys and Emoticons," later in this part.

Addresses

To send e-mail to someone, you need his or her address. Roughly speaking, mail addresses consist of the following elements:

+ Mailbox name, which is usually the user name of your account

+ @ (*at* sign)

+ Host name

For example, `elvis@ntw.org` is a typical address, where `elvis` is the mailbox name and `ntw.org` is the host name.

Mailbox names can contain the following elements:

+ Letters

+ Numerals

+ Some punctuation characters, such as periods and underscores

Capitalization normally does not matter in e-mail addresses.

Mailbox names should *not* contain the following:

+ Commas

+ Spaces

+ Parentheses

The most common situation in which these restrictions cause problems is with CompuServe addresses, which consist of two numbers separated by a comma. When converting a CompuServe address to an Internet address, change the comma to a period. For example:

> `71053,2615` becomes `71053.2615@compuserve.com`

If, for some reason, you must send mail to an address that does include commas, spaces, or parentheses, enclose the address in double quotes.

What's my address?

If you are accessing the Internet through a service provider, your address is most likely as follows:

`your.login.name@your.provider's.name`

If you are connected through work or school, your e-mail address is typically as follows:

`your.login.name@your.computer's.name`

A host name, however, is sometimes just a department or company name rather than your computer's name. If your login name is *elvis,* and your computer is `shamu.strat.ntw.org`, your mail address may be

`elvis@shamu.strat.ntw.org`
`elvis@strat.ntw.org`
`elvis@ntw.org`

or even

`elvis.presley@ntw.org`

If you're using a computer such as a PC or a Mac that isn't connected to the Internet all the time, your mail is probably handled by a central mail server. As a result, you should use your login name — the name you use when you contact the mail server.

If you're not sure what your mail address is, send a message to *Internet For Dummies* Central at `nidqr@dummies.com`, and we'll send back a note containing the address from which your message was sent, which is your mail address. While you're at it, add a sentence or two telling us how you like this book.

To find out someone else's e-mail address, *see* "Finding E-mail Addresses," later in this part.

Host names

Hosts are computers that are directly attached to the Internet.

Host names have several parts strung together with periods, like

`xuxa.iecc.com`

You decode a host name from right to left:

+ The rightmost part of a name is its *zone* (in the example, `com`).

+ To the zone's left (`iecc`) is the name of the company, school, or organization.

+ The part to the left of the organization name (`xuxa`) identifies the particular computer within the organization.

In large organizations, host names can be further subdivided by site or department.

A partial name is known as a *domain*. For example, `xuxa` is in the `iecc.com` and `com` domains. `iecc.com` is a *domain name*.

On the Internet, many names are valid only for mail.

In the U.S., host zone names are assigned by InterNIC and cost $100 to register and $50 per year after the first two years. For information about registering domain names, see this URL (see Part VI for what to do with a URL):

`http:/rs.internic.net/`

Host numbers

Network software uses the *host number,* which is sort of like a phone number, to identify the host. Host numbers are written in four chunks separated by periods, such as

```
140.186.81.6
```

The most important host number to know is the host number of the provider you use. Here's why:

+ You may need it to set up the software on your computer.

+ If things get fouled up, the number will help the guru who fixes your problem.

+ A few systems on the Internet don't handle names very well, so some users may need your number to contact you.

No particular relationship exists between host names and host numbers. A computer can have a host number but no host name — for example, a computer used by other computers, but not by humans. Also, a computer can have multiple host numbers if it's connected to multiple networks.

In case you are curious, host numbers consist of two parts:

+ The *network number* indicates the network that a host is connected to.

+ The *local host number* identifies the particular computer on that network.

Depending on the host's *class*, the first one, two, or three chunks of the number are the network number. The rest of the number is the local host number. The host's class is determined by the value of the first chunk. See the following table:

Class	First Chunk	Length of Network Number	Maximum Number of Hosts on Network
A	1-126	1 chunk	16,387,064
B	128-191	2 chunks	64,516
C	192-223	3 chunks	254

What does host number `140.186.81.6` mean? The first chunk (`140`) means that it is a Class B network; the network number, therefore, is in two parts: network `140.186`, host `81.6`.

Port numbers

Internet hosts usually can run many programs at once, and they can have simultaneous network connections to lots of other computers. The different connections are kept straight by *port numbers,* which identify particular programs on a computer. For example:

✦ File transfer (FTP) uses port 21.

✦ E-mail uses port 25.

✦ Usenet newsgroups use port 119.

Most of the time, programs automatically select the correct port to use. Now and then, however, a program uses a nonstandard port. In this book, we tell you the port number when we describe a program that uses a nonstandard port.

Zones

The *zone* is the last piece of the host name on the Internet (for example, the zone of dummies.com is com). Zone names come in two main kinds:

✦ Organizational

✦ Geographic

Organizational names

If the zone is three letters long, it is an *organizational name.* The three-letter code indicates the type of organization, and the part just before the zone indicates the specific organization.

Most systems that use organizational names are in the United States. The following table describes the organizational names that are currently used.

Zone	Type of Organization
com	Commercial organization
edu	Educational institution
gov	Government body or department
int	International organization (mostly NATO, at the moment)
mil	U.S. military site (can be anywhere)
net	Networking organization
org	Anything that doesn't fit elsewhere, such as a not-for-profit group

Geographic names

If the zone is two letters long, it is a *geographic name*. The two-letter code specifies a country, and the stuff in front of the zone is specific to that country. The us domain, used by some schools and small organizations in the United States, is set up strictly geographically. For example, John's machine in Cambridge, Massachusetts, is called chico.iecc.cambridge.ma.us.

A host can have more than one name. John's machine is also known as chico.iecc.com.

The following table lists popular geographic names. *See* Appendix A for a full list.

Zone	Country
at	Austria, Republic of
be	Belgium, Kingdom of
br	Brazil, Federative Republic of
ca	Canada
fr	France (French Republic)
jp	Japan
mx	Mexico (United Mexican States)
nl	Netherlands, Kingdom of the
no	Norway, Kingdom of
ru	Russian Federation
es	Spain, Kingdom of
se	Sweden, Kingdom of
ch	Switzerland (Swiss Confederation)
uk	United Kingdom
us	United States of America

Other zones

You may encounter a few other zones, including the following:

+ **arpa:** Left over from the ARPANET, the Internet's predecessor.

+ **bitnet:** Pseudozone used for mail to BITNET (another network).

+ **uucp:** Pseudozone used for mail to sites that use uucp, a crusty old network that uses dial-up modems.

America Online (AOL)

You can receive and send Internet mail by using your AOL account. If your AOL account name or screen name is `Steve Case`, your Internet address is `SteveCase@aol.com`. When you send mail from your AOL account, you can address it either to another AOL user (by typing the user's screen name) or to an Internet address (by typing the Internet address).

At the time this book was written, AOL's policy was not to charge for mail, including Internet mail.

Finding an address

To find the address of an AOL member, choose Members⇨Member Directory.

Reading incoming mail

1. Choose Mail⇨Read New Mail or click the You Have Mail icon on the Welcome window or the Read New Mail icon on the toolbar.

The New Mail window appears.

2. Highlight the message on the list.

3. Click Read or press Enter. AOL displays the message.

4. Click the Next icon to see the next message.

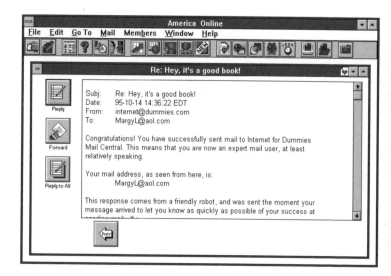

Sending new mail

1. Choose Mail⇨Compose Mail from the menu bar, or click the Compose Mail icon.

The Compose Mail window appears.

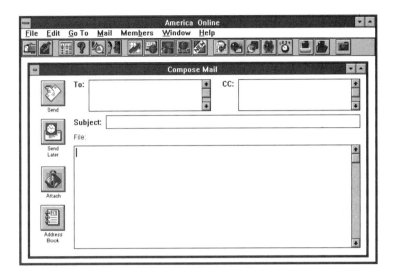

2. Type the recipient's address in the To box.

3. Type the addresses of anyone else you want to send this message to in the CC box.

4. Fill in the Subject line box.

5. Type your message in the main box.

6. After you're done, click Send Now or Send Later. Clicking Send Later holds your mail in an "outbox" for later transmission.

You can use the Tab key to go from box to box.

Replying to a message

1. While reading a message, click the Reply icon in the window that displays the message.

A mail window appears with the To box and the Subject line filled in. You can edit the subject, if you like.

2. Type your message in the main box.

3. After you're done, click the Send Now or Send Later button.

Forwarding a message

Forward

1. While reading a message, click the Forward icon in the message window.

A mail window appears with the To box and Subject line filled in. You can edit the subject if you want to.

2. Add a comment, if you like, in the main box.

3. After you're done, click the Send Now or Send Later icon.

Saving a message

1. Display the message you want on-screen.

2. Choose File⇨Save As.

3. Enter the filename you want to save this message under.

4. Select either Mail read or Text format, if AOL asks.

5. Click Save to save your message.

Reading saved messages

1. Choose File⇨Open.

2. Locate and open your mail directory or folder.

3. Select the message you want to read and click OK or press Enter.

Berkeley mail (UNIX systems)

Berkeley mail is the program that you run when you type the `mail` command on a UNIX shell account.

Reading incoming mail

1. Type **mail**.

mail lists your messages, marking the new ones with an *N*.

2. Press Enter to see the first message.

3. After you read the message, you can discard it (press d), reply to it (press r), forward it (*see* "Forwarding a message" in this section), or file it (press s). If you don't tell the program what to do with a message, the mailer either leaves the message in your mailbox or saves it to a file called `mbox`.

4. Press Enter to go to the next message.

5. When you're done, press q to quit after wiping out any messages you deleted or press x to exit without deleting anything.

TIP

If your mailer automatically saves messages in the mbox file, be sure to review and delete unneeded messages in your mailbox every so often.

Sending new mail

1. Type **mail** followed by the e-mail address of your recipient.

2. Enter an appropriate subject when asked.

3. Type the text of your message. Note that you can edit only the current line.

4. Type a period on a separate line or press Ctrl+D to end your message.

Replying to a message

1. After you read a mail message, press r to reply.

2. mail creates a new message addressed to the sender of the original message. The new message has the same subject as the original message.

3. Type the text of your reply the same way you enter a new message.

4. Type a period on a separate line or press Ctrl+D to end your message.

Forwarding a message

1. After you read a message, press m to create a new message.

2. Type the e-mail address to which you want to forward the message and press Enter.

3. Enter an appropriate subject when asked.

4. Type **~m** on a separate line to insert the original message.

5. Enter more text if you want.

6. Type a period on a separate line or press Ctrl+D to end your message.

The program responds with EOT (End of Text).

Saving a message

1. Display the message on-screen.

2. Press s (for *save*).

3. Type the name of a mailbox file and press Return.

mail appends the message to the mailbox file you selected. If the mailbox file does not exist, mail asks for confirmation.

Reading a saved message

Simply type **mail -f oldmailbox**. You can read all the messages in the file oldmailbox as though they were new mail.

Caveats

✦ Forging e-mail return addresses is not that hard, so if you get a totally off-the-wall message that seems out of character coming from that person, somebody else may have forged it as a prank.

✦ Many people on the Internet adopt fictional personas. The lonely flight attendant you are chatting up may be a 15-year-old boy. "On the Internet, no one knows you're a dog," says a cartoon in the *New Yorker*.

✦ E-mail is not very private. Not only can hackers read your mail as it passes from site to site, but so can your system administrator. Your employer may even have a legal right to read your mail at work. If you really need privacy, *see* "PGP" in Part XI.

✦ Be careful when forwarding mail. Some mail addresses are really mailing lists that redistribute messages to many other people.

✦ Not every mail address has an actual person behind it. Some are mailing lists (*see* Part V), and some are *robots* or *mailbots*. Mail robots have become popular as a way to query databases and retrieve files.

CompuServe

CompuServe is a commercial online service that can send and receive mail from the Internet. If your CompuServe ID is 77777,7777, then your Internet e-mail address is 77777.7777@compuserve.com (note that the comma within the ID number changes to a period). When you send mail from CompuServe to the Internet, add INTERNET: to the beginning of the address.

Note: This section assumes that you are using the CompuServe Information Manager program (WinCIM or MacCim) to access CompuServe.

Finding an address

To find the address of a CompuServe member, choose Mail⇨Member Directory from the menu.

Reading new messages

To get all your mail and read it offline, saving online charges while you read, follow these steps:

1. Choose Mail⇨Send/Receive All Mail/.
CompuServe gets your message.

2. Choose File⇨Disconnect.

3. Choose Mail⇨In Basket and double-click each message you want to read.

To read your mail online, click the Mail icon on the icon bar. A window listing your incoming messages, like the one in the following figure, appears. Double-click each message you want to read.

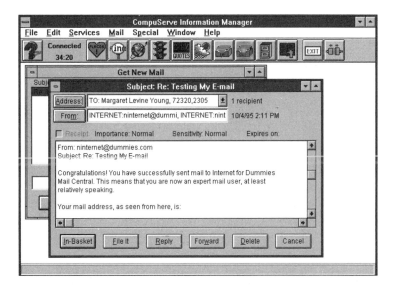

Sending new mail

1. Choose Mail⇨Create Mail. You see the Recipient List window.

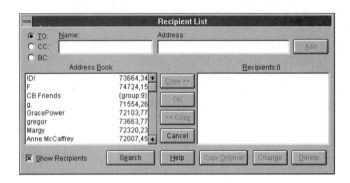

2. Type the recipient's name in the Name box.

3. Type the recipient's e-mail address in the Address box.

4. Click OK when you're done with the Recipient List window, and you see the Create Mail window. (MacCIM may skip this step.)

5. Fill in the Subject box.

6. Click the To or Address button to see your personal address book.

7. Click in the large text area and type your message.

8. (Optional) To attach a file, choose Mail⇨Send File.

9. Click either the Send Now or the Out Basket button. Clicking Out Basket holds your file for later transmission.

Sending a file

1. Choose Mail⇨Send File.

2. Choose the file you want to send.

3. Type the recipient's name in the Name box.

4. Type the recipient's e-mail address in the Address box.

5. Click OK to finish with the Recipient List window. You see the Send File Message window.

6. Fill in the Subject field.

7. Click the To or Address button to bring up your personal address book.

8. To attach the file, click the File button.

9. Click the Send Now button to send the file now, or click the Out Basket button to hold it and send it later.

Replying to a message

1. After you read the message, click the Reply button in the window that displays the message.

2. Type your reply.

3. Click either Send Now or Out Basket.

Forwarding a message

1. After you read a message, click the Forward button in the window that displays the message.

2. Enter the address of the person to whom the message should go.

If you want, add a comment or edit the forwarded text.

3. Click either Send Now or Out Basket.

Saving a message

After you read a message, click the File It button in the window that displays the message.

Reading saved messages

Your Filing Cabinet is a directory or folder on your hard disk where you can store e-mail messages and other information from CompuServe. To read the messages in the Filing Cabinet:

1. Choose Mail⇨Filing Cabinet.

2. Double-click the message you want to read.

elm (UNIX Systems)

The elm command runs a much nicer mailer than the usual mail command. For the complete story about elm, see *MORE UNIX For Dummies* (IDG Books Worldwide, Inc.).

Reading incoming mail

1. Type **elm**.

elm lists your incoming messages, marking new ones with an *N*.

2. Press Enter to see the first new message. If the message is more than one screen in length, press the spacebar to see each subsequent screen.

3. Press d to delete the current message and go on to the next. Or when viewing the last (or only) screen of the message, press the spacebar to go on to the next message without deleting the current one.

4. After you're done, press q to quit after wiping out any messages you deleted, or press x to exit without deleting anything. Either way, elm may ask you to confirm your choice.

You can see the list of subject lines again by pressing i (for *index*). To pick a message from the list, press the number shown on the line with the message. Or use the up- and down-arrow keys to move to the message and then press Enter to see the message.

Sending new mail

1. Type **elm**.

elm's main screen lists your incoming messages and displays a menu of commands.

2. Press m to send a message.

Alternatively, you can give elm the recipient's address when you run it. For example, you can type **elm king@ntw.org**.

3. elm asks you to enter a subject. Type one and press Enter.

4. elm may ask if you want to send copies to anyone. In the Copies to box, type any address to which you want to send a copy of the message and press Enter.

5. elm runs the standard local text editor, usually vi, pico, or emacs. Type the message, save the file, and exit the editor.

For more information about using vi, pico, and emacs, see *UNIX For Dummies*, 2nd Edition and *MORE UNIX For Dummies* (IDG Books Worldwide, Inc.).

6. elm responds by displaying a little menu. Choose e)dit message, !)shell, h)eaders, c)opy file, s)end, or f)orget.

7. Press s to send the message, or press f if you don't want to send it.

elm responds Mail sent! and then returns to the list of your incoming messages and a menu of commands.

Note: If you started elm with the recipient's name on the command line, elm just exits at this point.

8. To exit elm, press q. elm may ask you to confirm your choice. If so, press y to go ahead or n not to.

The editor you are using is often determined by a line in your .cshrc file in your home (login) directory. The line in the .cshrc file looks like:

```
setenv EDITOR vi
```

You can edit your .cshrc file and change this line to run the editor of your choice when you're creating e-mail.

Replying to a message

1. Display the message on-screen.

2. Press r.

elm asks whether to include a copy of the original message (which you can edit) in your reply.

3. Press y or n.

4. Edit the message and send the reply the same way you do a new message. ***See*** "Sending new mail," earlier in this section.

Forwarding a message

1. Display the message on-screen.

2. Press f to forward the message.

3. elm asks whether you want to edit the message before you forward it. Press y or n.

4. elm asks where you want the message forwarded to. Type the address.

5. Edit the message (if you pressed y in step 3), save the file, and exit the editor.

elm comes back with a little menu.

6. Choose e)dit message, !)shell, h)eaders, c)opy file, s)end, or f)orget.

If you press s, elm responds Mail sent! and then returns to the list of your incoming messages and a menu of commands.

Saving a message

1. Display the message on-screen.

2. Press s.

elm suggests a mailbox name based on the sender's name.

3. Press Enter to accept the suggestion, or type another mailbox name and then press Enter.

Reading a saved message

1. Press c (for *change* mailbox).

2. elm asks for the name of the mailbox. Enter it.

elm shows you a list of the messages in the mailbox. You can read them, reply to them, and so on just as if they were incoming messages.

3. To switch back to the list of incoming messages, press c again. When elm asks for the mailbox name, press ! (Shift 1).

4. elm may ask whether you want to save changes to the old mailbox; press y or n.

Etiquette

Sending electronic mail that seems rude or obnoxious is easy, even when you don't mean to. Here are a few suggestions regarding mail style:

+ Watch your tone. Your e-mail can seem brusque or rude even when you don't intend it to be.

+ Avoid foul language.

+ Don't *flame*. That is, don't send messages full of pointless and excessive outrage. For example:

```
What kind of stupid idiot thinks he can tell people
how to write their mail?
```

+ Double-check your humor — irony and sarcasm are easy to miss. Sometimes, it helps to add a *smiley* to let your reader in on the joke. For example:

```
What kind of stupid idiot thinks he can tell people
how to write their mail? :-)
```

✦ When in doubt, save your message overnight and read it again in the morning before you send it.

✦ If you do get involved in a vitriolic exchange of messages known on the Net as a *flame war,* the best way to stop is to let the other person have the last word.

✦ Your Subject line should tell the recipient as much as possible about your message, without getting too long. "Tonight's Softball Game is Canceled" is much better than "Important Announcement."

✦ Check your spelling. You may have to use a word processor if your mailer lacks a spell check feature.

✦ Remember, e-mail is not particularly private. A glitch can cause the system to deliver your mail to the wrong recipient on the wrong system (like your boss or your kids).

✦ Don't pass on chain letters like the following:

- The one about the dying boy who wants greeting cards (he doesn't)

- The "modem tax" rumor (the proposal was squelched in 1987)

- The "Good-news Virus" warning (a hoax)

- Any letter that offers you a way to make money fast by just putting your name at the bottom of the list and sending it to ten friends (These schemes are usually illegal, guaranteed to annoy your friends, and don't work for most suckers.)

See also *The Internet For Dummies,* 3rd Edition, Chapters 6 and 7.

Eudora (Windows and Mac)

There are two versions of Eudora: a simple "freeware" version — no charge — and a more complete commercial (but still inexpensive) version. Except where noted, we describe the freeware version.

Getting incoming mail

1. Choose File⇨Check Mail, or click the Check Mail icon on the toolbar.

Eudora dials up your account (if you are not already connected) and downloads any mail that you have to your PC.

2. If you have mail, Eudora displays a message and alerts you with a sound.

If you have the commercial version of Eudora, you can create "filters" that can automatically check incoming messages against a list of senders and subjects and file them in appropriate mailboxes.

Reading incoming mail

1. When Eudora loads, it displays its In folder, showing a list of all your mail, if you have any. If it doesn't display this list, choose Mailbox⇨In or click the In icon on the toolbar.

2. To read a message, double-click its line in the list.

   The message appears in a window.

Sending new mail

1. Choose Message⇨New message, or click the New Message icon on the toolbar.

   Eudora pops up a new message window.

2. Type the recipient's e-mail address on the To line.

3. Press Tab to skip to the Subject line.

4. Press Tab a few more times to skip the Cc and Bcc lines (or type the addresses of people who should get carbon copies and blind carbon copies of the message).

5. In the large area, type your message.

6. To send the message, click the button in the upper-right corner of the window, which, depending on how Eudora is configured, is marked Send or Queue.

If you click Send, Eudora sends the message immediately. If you click Queue, your message is stashed in your Outbox folder for transmission later, when you connect to your Internet provider.

Replying to a message

1. After reading a message, choose Message⇨Reply, or click the Reply icon on the toolbar.

Eudora pops up a message window with the recipient's address filled in and the recipient's message displayed. Each line of the original message appears in the message box, preceded by a > character.

2. Type your reply. It is good form to edit the original message so that only the important parts remain.

3. To send the message, click the button in the upper-right corner of the window labeled Send or Queue.

Forwarding a message

1. After reading a message, choose Message⇨Forward, or click the Forward icon on the toolbar.

Eudora pops up a message window with the current message displayed. Each line is preceded with a > character.

If you don't want the > characters, choose Message⇨Redirect To instead.

2. Type the recipient's e-mail address.

3. Edit the original message or add more text if you want.

4. To send the message, click the Send or Queue button in the upper-right corner of the window as you do when sending a new message.

Saving a message

1. Select the message by bringing its window to the front or by clicking its line in the In window.

2. Choose Transfer from the menu, and then choose a mailbox from the Transfer menu.

You can create additional mailboxes by choosing Transfer⇨New.

Reading saved messages

1. Select the mailbox that contains the messages(s) you want to read from the Mailbox menu.

2. Double-click the message on the window that appears.

eWorld

eWorld is Apple Computer's online service. It's designed for Macintosh users, who are a bit neglected by the other commercial online services. If your eWorld account is called TheWoz, then your e-mail address is TheWoz@eworld.com.

Reading incoming mail

1. Choose Unopened Mail from the eMail menu, or click the mail truck that appears when you have new mail.

2. Select the message you want to read and then click Open.

3. If a file is attached to a message you receive, click Get File Now to save it right away, or click Get File Later to add it to your list of files to get later.

Sending new mail

1. Choose eMail⇨New Message.

2. Enter the eWorld name of the recipient.

3. Fill in the Subject line.

4. Click in the large message field and type your message.

5. If you are connected, you can click Send Now to send the message immediately; clicking Send Later puts the message in your Out Box.

6. To send mail in the Out Box, choose eMail⇨Send Mail in Out Box to send it right away, or choose eMail⇨Automatic Courier to send it at a time you select.

The Internet, Fax, and Postal buttons let you send your message to an Internet address, as a fax, or as paper mail.

Attaching a file to a mail message

1. Click Attach File in the message window.

2. In the window that appears, select the items you want to send, and then click Attach.

TIP

Use the Compress Files option to compress files for faster transmission. If you attach more than one item, eWorld automatically compresses them.

Finding E-Mail Addresses

The biggest problem with e-mail is finding out someone's e-mail address. Right now, there is no perfect way to do so, but here are the best options:

✦ Keep an e-mail address book (a word processing file works fine). When someone sends you a message, copy the text in the message's From field and paste it in your electronic address book.

✦ Call the person on the telephone and ask.

✦ If you have the person's business card, see whether it lists an e-mail address.

✦ If you know or can guess the person's host name, use the `finger` command (not all providers offer `finger` service). *See* Part IX.

✦ All the commercial service providers have ways for you to look up the addresses of other subscribers to that service. But you have to be a subscriber on that provider's service. The address directory is one of the added values of a commercial service.

Several groups have set up Internet "white pages" directory services. None is close to complete. The following sections list the top four.

Four 11

SLED Corp.'s Four11 Online User Directory is an Internet white pages service that you can use to look for someone's e-mail address or home page. Anyone can be listed for free. If you use PGP encryption to keep others from reading your mail, Four11 will also certify and list your PGP key for a fee. *See* Part XI for information about PGP.

Try out the service, and at least register your address by using this URL:

```
http://www.Four11.com
```

Or send e-mail to `info@Four11.com`.

Netfind

InterNIC is the Internet Information Center for the U.S. part of the Net. InterNIC's Directory and Database Service, Netfind, searches a number of sources of directory information. It works best for finding people in universities and large corporations. To use it, go to this URL:

```
http://ds.internet.net/
```

Netfind also helps you find an Internet site anywhere in the world. Just specify the locale in your search.

Try different combinations. For example, if you are looking for Arnold Reinhold and know that he lives in Cambridge, Massachussetts, you might search for

```
reinhold cambridge
```

Unfortunately, this won't work because his Internet provider is in Brookline, not in Cambridge where he lives.

The Usenet database

M.I.T. keeps a database of everyone who has posted a message on a Usenet newsgroup. To search it, send e-mail to mail-server@rtfm.mit.edu with no subject line.

The message body should consist of the following line only:

```
send usenet-addresses/search-name
```

The *search-name* can contain as much information as you know about the person:

- ✦ firstname
- ✦ lastname
- ✦ login name
- ✦ host name
- ✦ city
- ✦ state
- ✦ country

whois

Whois is another database operated by InterNIC, but it contains mostly network administrator types and a few "notable" Net personalities. It is available at this URL:

```
http://ds.internet.net/
```

You will find two people named Reinhold, but not this author.

Headers

Headers are the lines of text that appear at the beginning of every Internet mail message.

Use following table as a guide to what these lines mean.

Header	Description
Subject:	Describes message (recommended)
To:	Lists recipients of the message (at least one required)
Cc:	Lists carbon copy recipients (optional)
Bcc:	Lists blind carbon copy recipients; these recipients names are not sent with message (optional)
From:	Address of message author (required, provided automatically)
Reply-To:	Address to send replies to if different than the From line (optional)
Date:	Time and date message sent (required, provided automatically)
Expires:	Date after which message expires (optional)
Message-ID:	Unique machine-generated identifier for message (required, provided automatically)
Lines:	Number text lines in message (optional, provided automatically)

Note: Many other optional header lines exist, but none of them is of great importance.

Mailers

To use e-mail, you need a mail program, or *mailer.* All mailers let you do the following:

- ✦ Read your incoming mail.
- ✦ Send new mail.
- ✦ Reply to messages you receive.
- ✦ Forward messages to other people via e-mail.
- ✦ Save messages for later.
- ✦ Read saved messages.

Many different mailers exist. Users of commercial online services such as Prodigy, CompuServe, and America Online can exchange mail with the Internet by using the standard mailers provided with those services.

This part of the book contains instructions for using the most popular Internet mailers: America Online, CompuServe, the Berkeley UNIX mail program, elm, eWorld, Eudora, and Pine. Each of these mailers is listed individually in alphabetical order.

Some Web browsers, like Netscape 2.0, can also read and send mail.

Netscape Navigator 2.0

Netscape Navigator 2.0 has integrated facilities for reading e-mail, similar to Eudora. It also allows e-mail that is "encrypted" for privacy. *See* "E-mail Security" in Part XI for more information.

Notification of Arriving Mail

When mail arrives, your system may try to tell you about it.

✦ Some systems display the message You have mail!

✦ Some systems make weird noises (boops, beeps, or even a rooster crowing).

✦ If there is a mail icon on your screen, it may change its appearance. Many systems display a country-style mailbox — when you have mail, the little red flag goes up and letters appear inside.

Pine (UNIX Systems)

The Pine mail program acts like a simplified elm; you send and read mail in a similar way.

Running Pine

1. To run Pine, type **pine**. You see the Pine main menu.

2. When you are done with Pine, press q to quit.

Pine asks whether you really, really want to quit.

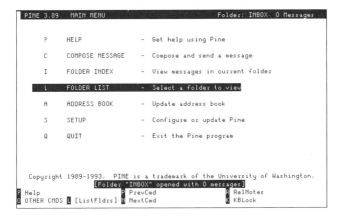

3. Press y to leave.

If you have left messages in your inbox that you have read but not deleted, Pine asks whether you want to move the messages to your read-messages folder — press y or n. If you deleted messages, Pine asks whether you really want to delete them. Again, press y or n.

Reading incoming mail

1. Press i to see the messages in the current folder, which is usually the Incoming folder.

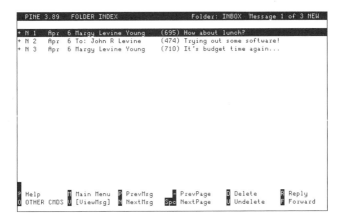

2. To read a message, move the highlight to it and press v or Enter.

3. To delete the current message, press d. To go on to the next message without deleting this one, press n.

4. After you're done, press m to return to the main menu.

Sending new mail

1. Press c to compose a message.

You see a blank message, like the following.

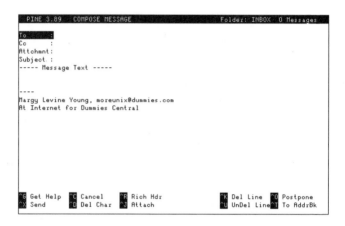

2. Enter the addresses and the subject line.

3. If you want to attach a file to a message, enter the filename in the Attchmnt: (attachment) blank.

4. Type the text of the message.

5. When you are ready to send the message, press Ctrl+X.

Pine asks if you really want to send the message.

6. Press y.

7. Press s to send the message. Press f if you don't want to send it.

Pine sends the message and displays the main menu again.

Replying to a message

1. Display the message on-screen.

2. Press r.

You see the same screen you see when composing a new message, with the address and subject filled in.

4. Edit the message and send the reply the same way you do a new message. *See* "Sending new mail" in this section.

Forwarding a message

1. Display the message on-screen.

2. Press f to forward the message.

You see the same screen you see when composing a new message, with the subject and text of the message filled in.

4. Edit and send the message the same way you do a new message. *See* "Sending new mail" in this section.

Saving a message

1. Display the message on-screen.

2. Press e.

Pine asks for the filename to save the message in (it puts the file in your home directory).

3. Enter the filename and press Enter.

Postmaster

Every Internet host that can send or receive mail has a special mail address called postmaster that is guaranteed to get a message to the person responsible for that host. If you send mail to someone and get back strange failure messages, you might try sending a polite message to the postmaster.

For example, if mail sent to king@bluesuede.org returns with an error, you might send e-mail to postmaster@bluesuede.org asking, "Does Elvis the King have a mailbox on this system? TIA, Ed Sullivan"

The postmaster is also the place to write if you believe that someone is seriously misusing a mail account. This is the Internet equivalent of reporting someone to the police, so use it judiciously.

Remember: The postmaster is usually an overworked system administrator, so it is considered poor form to pester him or her unnecessarily.

Prodigy

Prodigy is a commercial online service that can send and receive
e-mail from the Internet. If your Prodigy account is called ABCD123A,
your e-mail address is ABCD123A@prodigy.com.

Prodigy is constantly in the process of completely redesigning its
access programs, including its e-mail program. Your Prodigy software
may work differently from the way we describe it!

Reading incoming mail

If you have e-mail waiting for you, you see an envelope at the right
end of the toolbar (which appears at the bottom of the Prodigy
window). To read your messages:

> *1.* Select the envelope to go to Prodigy's e-mail area and see a list of
>   messages. Prodigy may run a separate mail program.

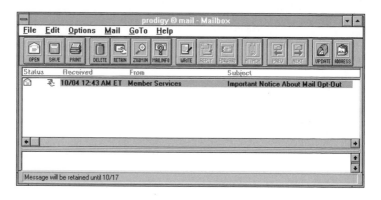

> *2.* Double-click a listed message to read it.

Sending new mail

> *1.* Type **Mail** or **Communication** in the Jump word box and press
>   Enter.

> *2.* Click Write (or Write a Message).
>
>   You see the Write window.

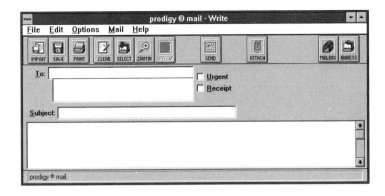

3. Type the recipient's Prodigy ID in the To box.

4. Fill in the Subject box.

5. Type your message in the large box.

6. Click the Send button.

Depending on your Prodigy service plan, you may be charged for each message!

Replying to a message

1. When you are reading a message, click the Reply icon on the toolbar, or choose Mail⇨Reply to Message.

Prodigy displays a new message window, with the address and subject lines already filled in. The original message appears at the bottom of the window.

2. Type your reply.

3. Click the Send button.

Forwarding a message

1. When you are reading a message, click the Forward icon on the toolbar, or choose Mail⇨Forward Message.

Prodigy displays a new message window, with the subject already filled in. The original message appears at the bottom of the window.

2. Type any additional message you want to include.

3. Click the Send button.

Finding an address

To find the address of a Prodigy member, type **Member List** in the Jump box.

Sending Mail to Folks with Accounts on Online Services

Many commercial online services have their own mail addressing schemes. The following table tells how to address Internet messages to these systems. In this table:

✦ *Username* is the name that the recipient uses to log onto the system.

✦ *Usernum* is the recipient's numerical user ID.

✦ *Hostname* is the name of the particular computer within the remote network.

System	How to Address Messages	Notes
America Online	*username*@aol.com	
Applelink	*username*@applelink.apple.com	Applelink is being phased out and replaced by eWorld.
AT&T Mail	*username*@attmail.com	
BITNET	*username*@hostname.bitnet **or** *username*%*hostname*.bitnet@mitvma.mit.edu **or** *username*%*hostname*.bitnet@cunyvm.cuny.edu	
BIX	*username*@bix.com	
CompuServe	*userid.userid*@compuserve.com	*userid.userid* is the numerical CompuServe ID with a period replacing the comma. For example, if the person's CompuServe ID is 71234,567, send mail to *71234.567@*compuserve.com.
Delphi	*username*@delphi.com	
Easylink	*userid*@eln.attmail.com	*userid* is the seven-digit user ID number.
eWorld	*userid*@eworld.com	
FIDO net	*firstname.lastname*@p4.f3.n2.z1.fidonet.org **or** *firstname.lastname*@f3.n2.z1.fidonet.org	Replace the numbers with parts of the person's Fido node number. For example, this user's Fido node number would be 1:2/3.4 or 1:2/3.

System	How to Address Messages	Notes
GEnie	*mailname*@genie.geis.com	*mailname* is based on the user's name, not the user's random login access name.
MCI Mail	*usernum*@mcimail.com	*usernum* is the person's numerical MCI mail address, usually written in the form 123-4567. Leave out the hyphen, though.
Prodigy	*usernum*@prodigy.com	The person's Prodigy account must be set up for Internet mail.
Sprintmail	/G=*firstname*/S=*lastname*/O=*orgname*/C=US/ADMD=TELEMAIL/@sprint.com	
UUCP	*username*@*hostname*.uucp or *hostname*!*username*@internet_gateway	The first UUCP form works only for registered addresses. The most common gateway is uunet.uu.net.

See also *The Internet For Dummies*, 3rd Edition, Chapters 5 and 6.

Smileys and Emoticons

Smileys, sometimes called *emoticons,* substitute for the inflection of voice that is missing in e-mail messages.

Smileys are still the e-mail equivalent of slang, so you probably shouldn't use them in a formal message at work.

Here are some common ones:

Smiley	What It Means
:-)	The basic smiley
;-)	Winking smiley; "Don't hit me for what I just said!"
:-(	Frowning smiley
:->	Sarcastic smiley
8-)	Wearing sunglasses
::-)	Wears glasses normally
:-(	Crying
;-)	So happy, I'm crying
:-@	Screaming
:-o	Uh oh!

(continued)

Smiley	What It Means
<g> or <grin>	Same as :-)
<sigh>	Sigh!
88	Love and kisses (from ham radio)
_\,/	I love you (from American Sign Language)
::	Action markers, as in ::picks up hammer and smashes monitor::

There are lots, lots more. You can check them out at either of the following URLs (*see* Part VI for what to do with a URL):

◆ The Smiley Dictionary

```
http://www.netsurf.org/~violet/Smileys/
```

◆ The EFF's Guide to Internet Smileys

```
http://www.germany.eu.net/books/eegtti/eeg_286.html
```

X.400

X.400 is a mail standard that competes with the Internet SMTP mail standard. Its main virtue is having been blessed by the U.N.'s International Communications Union, the same people who set the V.dot modem standards. In case you have to send mail to an X.400 system, here is a brief guide to X.400 addresses.

An X.400 address is more like a postal address than a phone number. It consists of a bunch of attributes. The most common attributes and the codes used to represent them are as follows:

◆ **Surname (S):** The recipient's last name

◆ **Given name (G):** The recipient's first name

◆ **Initials (I):** First or middle initial (or initials)

◆ **Generational qualifier (GQ or Q):** Jr., III, and so on

◆ **Administration Domain Name (ADMD or A):** More or less the name of the mail system

◆ **Private Domain Name (PRMD or P):** More or less the name of a private system gatewayed into a public ADMD

◆ **Organization (O):** The organization with which the recipient is affiliated

✦ **Organizational unit (OU):** The suborganization with which the recipient is affiliated

✦ **Country (C):** A two-letter country code; *see* Appendix A

✦ **Domain Defined Attribute (D, DD, or DDA):** Any code that identifies the recipient, such as user name or account number

You encode these attributes in an address, using / (a slash) to separate them and writing each attribute as the code, an equal sign, and the value.

Suppose, for example, that you want to send e-mail to Samuel Tilden at Tammany Hall in the United States by using Sprint's X.400 Sprintmail service, which is connected to the Internet via `sprint.com`. The address would be

```
/G=Samuel/S=Tilden/O=TammanyHall/C=US/ADMD=TELEMAIL/
   @sprint.com
```

One minor simplification applies if the only attribute needed is the recipient's actual name. Instead of writing

```
/G=Rutherford/I=B/S=Hayes/
```

you can simply write

```
Rutherford.B.Hayes
```

If someone tries to sell you a mail system based on X.400, throw that person out of your office.

X.500

X.500 is a standard for white-pages types of e-mail directory services from the same people who brought you X.400. It isn't quite as broken as X.400, and Internet people are trying to use it. When they have something that works, they'll tell you. Hopefully, you will never see what goes on inside.

For more information on using e-mail, see *Internet E-Mail For Dummies* (IDG Books Worldwide, Inc.).

Part IV

Usenet Newsgroups

Usenet newsgroups, also known as *Usenetwork news* or *Net-news,* is a worldwide, distributed bulletin board system. Internet users around the world submit Usenet messages, and within a day or so, these messages are delivered to nearly every other Internet host for everyone to read.

This part describes how to use the most common newsreaders, rn and trn.

In this part...

- ↙ **Frequently Asked Questions (FAQs)**
- ↙ **Newsgroup names**
- ↙ **News Netiquette**
- ↙ **Posting your first article**
- ↙ **Reading news with America Online**
- ↙ **Reading news with CompuServe**
- ↙ **Reading news with trn**
- ↙ **Reading news with Trumpet**
- ↙ **Starting your own newsgroup**

Reading Usenet is like trying to drink from a fire hose. Over 30,000 news articles — comprising over 150 megabytes of text — slosh through Usenet every day. Luckily, the articles are divided into *newsgroups* by topic. Here are some tips for maintaining your sanity:

+ Pick a few groups that really interest you.

+ Avoid the hot political groups unless you have an ample supply of Valium.

+ If you feel that you absolutely have to reply to a comment, save the message and sleep on it. If it still seems urgent in the morning, see "Posting Your First Article," later in this part.

+ Don't get into a *flame war*—an ongoing exchange of nasty messages—but if ever you do, let the other guy have the last word.

+ Don't believe everything you read in Usenet.

Frequently Asked Questions

Many newsgroups periodically post a list of frequently asked questions, or *FAQs*. They hope that you read the FAQs before posting a message that they have answered a dozen times before — and you should.

FAQs from all over Usenet are collected at a site called rtfm.mit.edu. (rtfm could stand for *Reference The FAQ Masters*. It usually means Read The, er, Fine Manual.) This site is, in effect, an online encyclopedia with the latest information on a vast array of topics.

You can access this site via FTP. *See also* Part VIII.

FAQs are usually quite authoritative, but sometimes they are just opinion. Reader beware!

Newsgroup Names

Usenet newsgroups have multipart names separated by dots, such as comp.dcom.fax (a group about fax machines). Related groups have related names. For example, groups that discuss data communication are all under comp.dcom.

The most popular Usenet newsgroup hierarchies are listed in the following table:

Newsgroup	Description
comp	Topics having something to do with computers; lots of meaty discussions
sci	Topics having something to do with one of the sciences, also meaty
rec	Recreational groups about sports, hobbies, the arts, and other fun endeavors
soc	Social groups — both social interests and plain socializing
news	Topics having to do with Net-news itself; a few groups with valuable general announcements, otherwise not very interesting
misc	Miscellaneous topics that don't fit anywhere else
talk	Long arguments, frequently political
alt	Semi-official "alternate" to the preceding newsgroup hierarchies (which are often called "the big seven"); alt groups range from the extremely useful to the totally weird

Regional and organizational hierarchies also exist:

Newsgroup	Description
ne	Topics of interest to New England
ny	For New York
ba	For the San Francisco Bay Area
ibm	For IBM
mit	For M.I.T.

New hierarchies are starting all the time, especially outside North America.

See also Appendix B for a more complete list of hierarchies.

Each system manager decides which newsgroups to receive and which to skip. The big providers get most of the newsgroups. On a UNIX system, you can see the list of newsgroups that are available on your system by typing

```
more /usr/lib/news/active
```

News Netiquette

The list of e-mail etiquette rules in Part III applies even more to posting news articles because *far* more people read news articles. Here are some additional rules:

✦ Don't post a follow-up to the whole group that is intended solely for the author of the original article. Instead, reply via e-mail.

✦ Be sure that each article is appropriate for the group to which you post it.

✦ Don't post a message saying that another message is inappropriate. The poster probably knows and doesn't care. For example, say someone posts an ad. Five other people post messages saying ads don't belong in that group. Several quote the original ad, others respond to those postings, and on it goes. The responses are far more disruptive than the single inappropriate ad. Silence is the best answer.

✦ If you want to complain about an article, send e-mail to the postmaster at the author's host. For example, if `joeblow@dummies.com` is harassing your newsgroup with offensive articles, send e-mail to `postmaster@dummies.com`.

✦ Make your subject line as meaningful as possible.

✦ If you are asking a question, use a question mark — for example, Subject: Meaning of Life?, *not* Subject: Meaning of Life.

✦ Don't post a two-line follow-up that quotes an entire 100-line article. Edit down the quoted material.

✦ Don't crosspost (that is, post the same article to multiple groups) unless you have a really good reason. Be especially careful when replying to multiple crossposted messages. Only post your reply to the newsgroups that will be interested.

✦ Watch out for *trolls* (messages calculated to provoke a storm of replies). Not every stupid comment needs a response.

✦ Most groups periodically post a list of Frequently Asked Questions (or *FAQs*). Read the FAQs before asking a question. *See also* "Frequently Asked Questions," earlier in this part.

Here are several classic messages that you should never post:

✦ "I saw something in a book once, but I don't have it here. I think it said . . ."

✦ "You shouldn't post that kind of message in `alt.foo.bar`."

✦ "You're an <expletive deleted>!"

✦ "This message isn't really about sex, but now that I've got your interest. . . ."

✦ "There is this dying kid, and before he dies, he wants . . ."

✦ "Here is how to make a lot of money fast. . . ."

See also "Posting Your First Article," the next section in this part.

Posting Your First Article

Standard Usenet dogma is to read a group for a few weeks before posting anything. This is still good advice, but Internet newbies generally aren't big on delayed gratification. So here's the general procedure for your first posting:

1. Pick a newsgroup whose subject is one you know something about.

2. Read the FAQs.

3. Reply to an article with specific information that you know first-hand or can cite in a reference and that is relevant to the topic being discussed.

4. Type a reply that is short, clear, and to the point.

5. Edit text included from the original article down to the bare minimum.

6. Use an appropriate distribution to keep local stuff local. Typical entries are *world, na* (North America), *usa, can* (Canada), *uk, ne* (New England), *nyc* (New York City), *la* (Los Angeles), and *ba* (San Francisco Bay area).

7. Edit the follow-up newsgroup list down to one or two groups.

Follow these guide lines when composing your message:

✦ Stay calm.

✦ Don't be inflammatory.

✦ Don't use foul language.

✦ Don't call people names.

✦ Your article should contain more than your opinion. Facts, pointers to more information, well thought-out and concise arguments, and good questions are always welcome.

✦ Read the entire preceding thread (all the articles on the same subject) to make sure that your point hasn't been raised already.

✦ Have your facts straight.

♦ Check your spelling.

♦ Double-check your grammar.

♦ Never criticize someone else's spelling or grammar.

♦ Don't use a lot of Netisms like ROTFL (an abbreviation for Rolling On The Floor, Laughing).

♦ If necessary, use one smiley :-).

♦ ***Remember:*** Save your message overnight and re-read it before posting it.

Some newsgroups are *moderated.* This means the following:

♦ Articles are not posted directly as news. Instead, they are e-mailed to a person who posts the article only if he or she feels that it's appropriate to the group.

♦ Moderators, who are generally unpaid volunteers, do not process items instantaneously, so it can take a day or two for items to be processed.

♦ If your article doesn't appear and you really don't know why, post a polite inquiry to the same group.

Reading News with America Online

America Online (AOL) allows you to both read and post to newsgroups.

Starting the AOL newsreader

1. Click the Internet Connection icon in the Main Menu window.

2. Click the News Groups icon in the Internet Connection window.

3. Click the Read My Newsgroups icon in the Newsgroups window. Or you can go to the keyword *newsgroups.*

You see your personalized list of *newsgroups.* AOL starts you out with a handful of groups, including news.announce.newusers, news.answers, news.groups.reviews, and some AOL help groups.

4. Double-click the group you want to read.

AOL tries to shield you from the cryptic Usenet names by translating them into "English." But it provides an icon labeled Internet Names that lets you see a group's real name. Unfortunately, you have to switch back to the English names to do any work.

You see a list of threads (conversations) in your selected newsgroup.

5. Double-click a thread to start reading it.

Posting a follow-up article

To post an article following up on a displayed message:

1. Click the Reply to Group button. You see a Reply to Author window.

2. Fill in the Response field.

3. Click Send.

AOL offers you a Copy Author of original message via EMail check box. This is usually a welcome courtesy, so do check it.

AOL does not let you edit the list of newsgroups to which your article will be posted.

Posting a new article

1. When the window listing messages for the newsgroup that you want is displayed (*see also* "Going to a newsgroup," earlier in this section), click the Send New Message icon. You get a Post New Message window.

2. Fill in the Subject line carefully. *See also* "News Netiquette," earlier in this part.

3. Type the message.

4. Re-read your message carefully.

5. Click the Send button.

Reading News with CompuServe

Starting the CIS newsreader

1. Click the Internet icon in the Services window.

(This window is also called the Basic Services or Browse window, depending on which version of WinCIM or MacCIM you use to connect to CompuServe.)

2. Click the Usenet Newsgroups icon in the Internet window.

3. Double-click the Usenet newsreader (CIM) line in the Navigating window. (CIM stands for *CompuServe Information Manager*.)

4. Double-click the Access Your Usenet Newsgroups line in the Usenet Newsgroups window.

If the Access Your Usenet Newsgroups line is grayed out, it means that you have not yet subscribed to any groups. *See also* "Subscribing to newsgroups," later in this section.

You see your personalized list of newsgroups.

5. Double-click the group you want to read.

You see a list of threads — groups of messages with the same subject line — in your selected newsgroup.

6. Click a thread and then click the Get button to start reading it.

You can click all the threads or messages you plan to read and then Click the Retrieve button to download them en masse.

Leaving the newsreader

To leave the WinCIM or MacCIM newsreader, keep clicking Cancel buttons until you see the general WinCIM or MacCIM window.

Then choose File⇨Leave.

Going to a newsgroup

1. Start the CompuServe Information Manager (CIM) program by double-clicking its icon.

2. Click the Internet icon in the Services window.

3. Click the Usenet Newsgroups icon in the Internet window.

4. Double-click the Usenet newsreader (CIM) line in the Navigating window.

5. If you find graphical interfaces and mice difficult to use, try clicking the Usenet newsreader (ASCII) line in the Navigating window.

6. Double-click the Subscribe to Newsgroups line in the Usenet Newsgroups window.

You see a list of the most popular Usenet hierarchies. *See also* "Newsgroup Names," earlier in this part.

CIM lets you quickly find newsgroups by typing a word or phrase in the Keyword box and clicking the Search button.

7. Double-click one of the hierarchies to get a list of all the newsgroups in that hierarchy along with any subhierarchies.

A newsgroup with many levels (for example, alt.music.folk. lavin.concerts.ca) requires a number of steps to get to. Just keep clicking.

8. When you get to a newsgroup you want to read, click the Preview button, and you get a list of available threads.

9. Double-click a thread to read its messages.

When you leave the group, CIM asks whether you want to subscribe to that group.

Subscribing to a newsgroup

To add a newsgroup to your personalized list, follow the steps in "Going to a newsgroup," in this part. When you find a group that you want, highlight it and then click the Subscribe button.

WinCIM and MacCIM thoughtfully provide check boxes next to the name of each newsgroup. Check the ones that you want and click the Subscribe button after you're done.

If you know the newsgroup's Usenet name, click the Subscribe By Name button in the Subscribe to Newsgroups window. You can then type the name and click OK.

CompuServe does not list some groups, apparently because their title or content may be offensive.

If you know the name of such a group, you can still visit it by clicking the Subscribe By Name button and typing the name.

Parental control

Unlike AOL, CompuServe just warns you to watch what your kids are up to. (Like you know more than they do?)

Unsubscribing to a newsgroup

1. Double-click the Subscribe to Newsgroups line in the Usenet Newsgroups window.

2. Highlight the newsgroup that you want to drop.

3. Click the Remove button.

Saving an article

While the article is on-screen, choose File⇨Save or File⇨Save As.

Junking and killing an uninteresting article

When a list of threads (or messages) is displayed, you can highlight one or more and click the Clear button to delete them from the list.

Replying to an article

To reply to a displayed message:

1. Click the Reply button. You see a Reply to Usenet Message window.

WinCIM and MacCIM give you a choice of Sending via E-mail or Posting to Newsgroup. When in doubt, just send e-mail.

2. Fill in the Message Contents field.

3. Re-read your message carefully.

If you are posting your reply, review the list of newsgroups in the upper-right corner. If several groups are listed, consider removing some of them by unchecking the box next to the group's name. *See also* "Newsgroup Names," earlier in this part.

If you are posting your reply, send the author a copy by checking the Send via E-mail check box, too. This is usually a welcomed courtesy.

It is standard practice to put the characters **Re:** in front of the subject field in a reply, but CIM doesn't do so automatically. (When replying to replies, **Re: Re:** or **Re2:** is overkill.)

Posting a new article

1. When the window listing messages for the newsgroup you want is displayed, click the Create button.

You get a Create Usenet Message window.

2. Fill in the Subject line carefully. *See* "News Netiquette," earlier in this part.

3. Type the message contents.

4. Re-read your message carefully.

5. Check the Post to Newsgroup box.

6. Click the Send button.

You can also send a copy of the message via e-mail by checking that box as well. Perhaps your mother saves all your postings.

Extracting binary files

Some newsgroups feature messages that contain graphics or other nontext files encoded as text so that they can be posted in Usenet articles. For example, read the alt.binaries.pictures.fractals to see lots of cool fractal pictures. WinCIM and MacCIM extract most binary files, such as images, from encoded messages.

Reading News with trn (UNIX Systems)

Several programs help you read Usenet newsgroups on UNIX systems. The most widely used is trn. An older program called rn is also used. It is similar to trn, but it lacks thread support.

Starting the trn newsreader

To start the newsreader, type **trn** at the UNIX prompt.

The first time you run trn, it does some automatic setup:

```
% trn
Trying to set up a .newsrc file—running newsetup...
Creating .newsrc in /usr/john1 to be used by news
    programs.
Done. If you have never used the news system before,
    you may find the articles
in news.announce.newusers to be helpful.  There is also
    a manual entry for rn.
To get rid of newsgroups you aren't interested in, use
    the 'u' command.
Type h for help at any time while running rn.
Unread news in general          14 articles
(Revising soft pointers—be patient.)
Unread news in ne.food          47 articles
Unread news in ne.forsale       1177 articles
Unread news in ne.general       268 articles
Unread news in ne.housing       248 articles
etc. ********  14 unread articles in general—read now?
    [+ynq]
```

trn keeps track of the newsgroups that you are interested in — that is, those that you are *subscribed to.* If you are not interested in a newsgroup, you can *unsubscribe.* When new newsgroups are created, trn asks whether you want to subscribe to them.

When you use trn for the first time, it assumes that you are subscribed to all newsgroups. You must unsubscribe to those you don't care about.

You can't read everything on Usenet. Don't even think of trying.

Selecting newsgroups

The following table contains a list of commands that you use when selecting newsgroups.

You usually don't need to press Enter (or Return) after single-letter commands. However, some commands require that you type a line of text *after* the letter, such as a filename or a newsgroup name. In that case, you do press Enter to indicate that you're done with the line of text.

Command	Description
Spacebar or y	Enter the next group that has unread news (*see also* "Reading the messages in a newsgroup," in this section).
n	Skip this group for now (*see also* "Skipping over newsgroups," in this section).
u	Unsubscribe from this group so that you don't see it anymore (*see also* "Unsubscribing to a newsgroup," in this section).
g	Go to a group; type the group name after the g (*see also* "Finding a newsgroup," in this section).
q	Quit trn.
p	Go to the previous group with unread news.

Press h for a list of these and other options.

Entering a newsgroup

To enter a newsgroup, press the spacebar when trn asks whether you want to read the messages in that group. trn shows you the first screen of the first unread message or *article* in the group.

You can

+ Read each article that you haven't read yet.

+ Skip over articles that look boring.

+ Reply to messages by e-mail.

+ Post a follow-up article.

+ Save the article.

To read the messages in a newsgroup, press the spacebar when `trn` asks whether you want to read them.

You see the first message that you have not yet read, something like

```
general #6281          (1)
From: root-Admin(0000)        (1)
[1] Disk space         (1)
Organization: I.E.C.C.        (1)
Date: Sat Aug  7 06:48:03 1996       (1)
+                      [1]
The disks are nearly full again. Please delete unneeded
    files, or we'll delete some for you.
(Yes, that's a threat.)
—
Your friendly system manager
End of article 6281 (of 6282)—what next? [npq]
```

The last line tells you how many articles have been posted in the newsgroup (*6282*) and which one you are looking at again (*6281*). It also asks what you want to do next. You can press the keys in the following table:

Key	Description
Spacebar	View the next screen of the message, much like the more UNIX command (in fact, it *is* the more UNIX command).
n	Go on to the next article.
q	Quit this newsgroup and go on to the next one.
c	"Catch up" — that is, pretend that you've read all the articles.

Once you get the hang of it, you'll mostly press the spacebar to go to the next article or newsgroup, press n to skip an article or newsgroup, and press k to skip a group of articles (described in the next section).

Reading articles

Here is a summary of keystrokes for reading articles:

Spacebar	Read the next page of the current article or the next unread article.
n	Skip to the next article.
k	Kill this article and any others with the same title.
K	Same as *k,* but also enter the title in your kill file so the title is *rekilled* each time you enter the group.
q	Leave this group.
c	Catch up (pretend that you've read all articles in this group).
u	Unsubscribe to this newsgroup.
s *file*	Save article to a file named *file.*
lpr	Print the article (don't use this if you are logged in remotely!).
/*xyz*	Find the next article whose title contains *xyz.*
=	Show titles of unread articles.
Ctrl+R	Restart the current article (redisplays the first page).
X	Unscramble message ciphered with *rot-13,* a simple code used mostly for off-color jokes.
e	Extract uuencoded or shar file (**see also** "Extracting binary files," in this part).

Press h for a list of these and other options.

Leaving the newsreader

When you are bored of reading messages from computer nerds all over the world, it's time to exit your newsreader: Press q.

Depending on where you are in the program, you may have to press q two or three times.

Going to a newsgroup

To read the messages of a particular newsgroup, use the g (*goto*) command. For example, type **g rec.pets.cats** at the trn prompt.

If you have unsubscribed to a group and want to turn it back on, the g command turns it back on.

You can start trn in a specific newsgroup by typing **trn rec.pets.cats**, for example at the UNIX prompt.

UNIX commands let other users see what commands you are executing. You may not want everyone to know you entered `trn` `alt.sex`. For privacy, start `trn` without specifying a newsgroup. Then use the `g` command to go to the one you want.

Skipping over newsgroups

When `trn` asks whether you want to read a newsgroup now, you can skip over it just this once but remain subscribed to the newsgroup. Just press n to say no, don't read it now.

Unsubscribing to a newsgroup

When `trn` asks whether you want to read a newsgroup, you can *unsubscribe* — that is, tell it that you never want to hear about the newsgroup again. Press u, and you won't see the group at all in the future.

Don't worry, you can resubscribe with the `g` command. ***See also*** "Going to a newsgroup," in this section.

Ordering newsgroups

You can tell `trn` to present the most interesting newsgroups first so that you can move quickly through your favorite groups by pressing the spacebar or n.

To change the order of your newsgroups, press m (*for move*) and do one of the following:

◆ If you want to move the current group, press Enter. To move some other group, type the group's name followed by Enter.

◆ To move the group to the end of the list so that it's the last one you see, type $.

◆ To move the group to the beginning of the list so that it's the first one you see, type ^ (a caret, usually Shift+6).

◆ To move the group to appear after another group, type +, type the name of the other group, and then press Enter.

To see a list of all the groups you subscribe to (or have ever subscribed to) press L (uppercase). To see a list of groups you *don't* subscribe to, press l (lowercase).

Put the newsgroups you read regularly at the top of the list.

`trn` keeps track of the order of newsgroups in a file called `.newsrc`. If you feel confident, you can edit this file with a text editor to reorder it. Save a copy of `.newsrc` before you start, in case you mess up.

See our *UNIX for Dummies*, 2nd Edition, (IDG Books Worldwide, Inc.) for how to edit a file in UNIX.

New newsgroups

Because Usenet is still growing, dozens of mostly useless new newsgroups appear every day. If any new ones have appeared since you last ran `trn`, you are told about them (whether you like it or not!) when you start `trn`:

```
INewsgroup alt.comp.hardware.homebuilt not in .newsrc—
    subscribe? [ynYN]
```

Press y if you want to subscribe; otherwise, press n.

If you press y, `trn` then asks:

```
Put newsgroup where? [$^.Lq]
```

The possible answers you can give are

- ✦ **^:** Puts the newsgroup first

- ✦ **$:** Puts the newsgroup last

- ✦ **.(period):** Puts the newsgroup before the current newsgroup

- ✦ **+newsgroup name:** Puts the newsgroup after the indicated current newsgroup

- ✦ **L:** Gives a listing of newsgroups you subscribe to

- ✦ **q:** If you change your mind and don't want to subscribe

Press h for a list of these and other options. Press N (capital N) if you don't want to subscribe to any new groups now.

Selecting the threads you want to read

So many articles are in a newsgroup that you may want to select only those subjects that you *do* want to see. `trn` has a feature called *thread selection* that makes the selection easy (`rn` doesn't have this feature). A thread is a group of articles with the same subject line.

Enter the desired newsgroup by pressing + or spacebar (rather than y). You see something like this:

```
Reading overview file.
news.announce.newgroups        91 articles (moderated)

a  Kenneth Herron   1  CFV: comp.lang.java
b  Bill Aten        1  CFV: rec.knives
d  Robert Haas      1  CFV: soc.culture.south-africa.afrikaans
e  Gerald Mesaric   1  RFD: comp.infosystems.hyperg
f  Bob Stout        1  RFD: comp.lang.c.code
g  John Fitch       1  RFD: comp.music.reorganization
I  Jason Newquist   1  RFD: comp.sys.mac.programmer.games
j  Mark Odegard     1  RFD: misc.health.syndromes.tourette
l  Brent E. Boyko   1  RFD: rec.music.makers.choral
o  Ilana Stern      1  RFD: rec.travel.caribbean
r  Marcus Monnig    1  RFD: soc.culture.pacific-island
s  Ilana Stern      1  2nd RFD: misc.consumers.frugal-living
t  Jan Isley        1  CFV: comp.lang.perl.tk
u  Kenneth Herron   1  CFV: comp.sys.ibm.pc.games.sports
v  Dave Cornejo     1  CFV: humanities.design.misc
w  Robert Haas      1  CFV: misc.business.credit.moderated
x  Bill Aten        1  CFV: misc.health.therapy.occupational
y  Bill Aten        1  CFV: misc.news.internet.{announce,discuss}
z  Michael Handler  1  CFV: news.admin.censorship
```

The preceding screen example is a "table of contents" for the newsgroup, listing the threads (with a one-letter identifier), author, number of articles in the thread, and subject.

+ Select the threads you want by pressing the appropriate letter. To select a range of threads, press the letter of the first one, followed by a hyphen, and then the letter of the last thread.

+ To go to the next page of threads, press > (right arrow).

+ To start reading the threads you've selected, press Z or Tab.

+ If you want to read all the threads on the current screen, simply press Z or Tab without selecting any of them.

+ To junk the threads that aren't selected, press D.

The most effective way to pick just the articles of interest is to select the interesting threads on each screen by using the key letters and then press D to quickly skip the rest of the threads on that screen.

Pressing the spacebar at the end of each screen picks the command that you are most likely to want:

✦ If there is another screen of threads, pressing the spacebar does the same thing as > (goes to the next screen).

✦ On the last screen, spacebar is the same as Z (to start reading articles).

The following table summarizes key letters that are useful in thread selection:

Key	Meaning
Spacebar	Read the next page of the table of contents or start reading selected articles if no more threads are in the table of contents.
D	Start reading selected articles and mark unselected articles as read.
Z	Read selected articles.
/xyz	Select articles whose titles contain *xyz*.
c-g	Select articles *c* through *g* in the current table of contents.
c	Catch up by pretending that you've read every article in the group (recent versions of t rn only).
h	Show extremely concise help.
q	Leave this group.

Saving an article

To save an article you are reading, press s followed by the name of the file in which to save it. If you don't specify a directory, articles are saved in your directory News — usually as good a place as any.

If the file doesn't already exist, t rn asks whether it should make the file a mailbox. Press y. If you save multiple articles in a mailbox-format file, you can use any of the UNIX mail programs discussed in Part II to read the file. Otherwise, your articles are saved in one big text file.

Junking and killing an uninteresting article

Often, you find an article to be uninteresting enough that you want to skip it, all the replies, and perhaps every future reply as well.

✦ To skip (kill) this article and all others with the same subject, press k (lowercase).

✦ To kill this subject permanently and skip it in the future as well, press K (uppercase).

✦ To skip (junk) the rest of this thread (a group of messages on a single topic) even if the subject changes, press J (uppercase).

Posting a follow-up article

You can respond to an article in one of two ways:

✦ You can send e-mail to the article's author. ***See also*** "Replying to an article by e-mail," later in this section.

✦ You can write an article of your own to the network at large.

To post a follow-up article:

1. While reading the original article, press f (lowercase) to send a follow-up. If you want to include some or all of the text of the article in your follow-up, press F (uppercase) instead.

If you press f, trn asks

```
Are you starting an unrelated topic? [ynq]
```

Press n.

2. trn asks if you're sure that you want to send a follow-up to the whole Net. Press y.

trn starts a text editor with a skeleton of the follow-up message already provided. If you pressed F, it includes a copy of the original article.

3. Type your follow-up.

If you started with the original article, *please, please, please* edit out the irrelevant parts.

4. Save the file and leave the editor. trn asks whether you want to send, abort, edit, or list the response.

5. To see what you are about to send, press l. To make any changes, press e. To send the message, press s. If you changed your mind, press a to send nothing.

Always press l and read what you are about to post before pressing s.

All news articles that you send, including follow-ups, automatically add your signature file. So don't put in the signature yourself, or it'll appear twice.

Posting a new article

Be sure to read "Posting Your First Article," earlier in this part, for tips regarding when it's a good idea to start posting to Usenet newsgroups.

1. Within trn, enter the newsgroup of interest.

   If you're in the thread-selection screen, press > to get to the article-reading screen.

2. Press f (as though you were writing a follow-up article to the current article).

   trn asks

   ```
   Are you starting an unrelated topic? [ynq]
   ```

3. Press y.

   trn asks for a distribution code. usa keeps it in the U.S.; just press enter for worldwide distribution of your article.

4. When you are prompted to do so, enter a new subject for the article.

5. trn then asks if you're sure you want to do this. Press y.

6. Write the new article the same way you'd write a follow-up (described in "Posting a follow-up article").

7. Re-read your article carefully before sending it. *See also* "Posting Your First Article," earlier in this part.

Replying to an article by e-mail

You can respond to an article in one of two ways:

✦ You can send e-mail (known as a *reply*) to the article's author. Send a reply by e-mail unless you are sure that your response will be of interest to most of the people in the newsgroup.

✦ You can write an article of your own (known as a *follow-up*) to the network at large. *See also* "Posting a follow-up article."

To send an e-mail reply:

1. While reading the original article, press r (lowercase). If you want to include some or all of the text of the article in your reply, press R (uppercase) instead.

   trn or rn starts a text editor (usually vi, pico, or emacs), with a skeleton of the reply message already provided. If you press R, it includes a copy of the original article. *See UNIX for Dummies*, 2nd Edition for more information on how to use vi, pico, and emacs.

2. Type in your reply. If you started with the original article (R), please edit out the irrelevant parts.

3. Save the file and leave the editor (^**X** in pico; **:wq** in vi).

t r n asks whether you want to send, abort, edit, or list the response.

4. To see what you are about to send, press l. To make any changes, press e. To send the message, press s. If you changed your mind, press a to send nothing.

t r n also asks if it should add your standard signature (stored in your signature file).

5. Press y unless you already signed the article.

Extracting binary files

Some articles contain encoded binary data, such as pictures or executable programs. Such messages look like this:

```
begin plugh.exe 644
M390GNM4L-REP3PT45G00I-05[I5-
    6M30ME,MRMK760PI5LPTMETLMKPY
MEOT39I4905B05YOPV30IXKRTL5KWLJROJTOU,6P5;3;MRU05OI4J5OI4
```

(This is called *uuencoded* format.) These messages usually appear in newsgroups dedicated to distributing graphics, sound, video, and software (these newsgroups frequently contain the word *binary* in their names).

Before you can use this information, you must *extract*, or *uudecode*, it.

✦ Press e followed by Enter. If you want the data someplace other than your News directory, type the directory name after the **e**.

✦ If the file is large and is split across multiple messages, press e in each message in order.

Other news programs

You can use several other popular news programs for UNIX systems, notably nn and t i n. ***See*** *Internet Secrets* (IDG Books Worldwide, Inc.) for lots of hints on using nn.

Reading News with Trumpet

Trumpet is a popular newsreader for Macintosh and PC users with SLIP (or PPP) Internet accounts. Peter R. Tattam of the University of Tasmania wrote Trumpet and distributes it as shareware. If you like it, send $40 (in U.S. dollars) to him at Trumpet Software International, GPO Box 1649, Hobart, Tasmania, Australia 7001.

In order to get newsgroup information, your SLIP provider must run a special protocol called NNTP so that Trumpet can tap into it. The computer that runs NNTP is called your *news server*. Your provider should be able to help you get Trumpet up and running. (We sure can't.)

Starting Trumpet

Double-click the Trumpet icon.

You see a "guilt" screen asking for your shareware fee. The best way to avoid seeing this message every time is to send in your money.

The first time you run Trumpet, you need to fill in a startup screen with a lot of information about your SLIP provider, like the Internet address of your provider's news server. Get this information from your provider ahead of time. (Just say, "Tell me everything I need to know to get Trumpet running.") Here is some information that you'll need:

News host name	The name of your news server
Mail (or POP) host name	The name of your mail (or post office) server
Your e-mail address	E-mail address — just what it sounds like
Organization	The name of the organization that you work for, or whatever you want to appear in your messages (for example, "Pat's gerbil farm dis-")
Signature file name	The name of a file that contains your signature
POP user name	Your user name on the POP system

If you don't get it all right the first time, choose File⇨Setup anytime you want to make corrections.

Leaving the newsreader

Choose File⇨Exit (or Quit).

Going to a newsgroup

1. Access the News Viewer window, which shows a list of the newsgroups to which you are subscribed.

When you run Trumpet for the first time, this list is tremendously long, and you can see only the first few entries. *See also* "Subscribing and unsubscribing to newsgroups," in this section.

2. Select a newsgroup by double-clicking it.

Trumpet asks your news server for its articles. This process can take a few minutes for a large newsgroup.

Finally, you see a list of the articles in the newsgroup, showing the author, size in lines, and subject of each article.

3. To read an article in the list, double-click it.

Subscribing and unsubscribing to newsgroups

1. Choose Groups Subscribe from the menu bar.

You see the Subscribe to News Groups window.

2. Choose a hierarchy from the Top level Hierarchy list. ***See also*** "Newsgroup Names," at the beginning of this part.

The Subscribed groups box fills with a list of the groups in that hierarchy that you are already subscribed to. The Unsubscribed groups box contains a list of those that you are not subscribed to.

- To subscribe to a newsgroup in the Unsubscribed group box, just click it. It jumps into the Subscribed groups box.

- Conversely, to unsubscribe to a newsgroup in the Subscribed group box, click it. It disappears from your Subscribed group list and appears in the Unsubscribed group list.

Keep choosing different hierarchies, and sorting through the groups, subscribing and unsubscribing as you go.

3. After you're done, click OK.

To unsubscribe to one group quickly, select it from the newsgroups list and choose Groups Unsubscribe from the menu bar.

After doing a lot of work on your list of subscribed newsgroups, it is a good idea to exit Trumpet and run it again. Doing so saves your list of groups, just in case disaster strikes.

Saving an article

Choose Article⇨Save to save the entire text of the article in a text file.

Replying to an article by e-mail

1. View the article to which you want to respond.

2. Click the Reply button.

You see the Mail Article window.

Trumpet fills in the address of the person you are responding to, the subject, and your address automatically.

3. Type the text of your message.

Trumpet includes the full text of the original article. Edit the text to include only the part of the article that you want to respond to and delete all other unnecessary text.

4. Double-click the close box Control-menu box in the upper-left corner of the window to close it. (Single-click on a Mac.)

Trumpet then asks if you want to cancel this electronic mail:

- To send the message, click the No button.

- To cancel it, click Yes. (Sigh.)

- To return to editing your message, click Cancel.

Posting a follow-up article

1. View the message to which you want to respond publicly.

2. Click the Follow button.

Trumpet displays the Post Article window. Trumpet automatically fills in the name of the newsgroup that you are reading, the same subject and keywords used by the article you are replying to, and the suggested distribution.

3. Type the text of your article. Make it concise and clear, and check your grammar and spelling.

Trumpet includes the full text of the original article. Edit the text to include only the part of the article you want to respond to, and delete all other unnecessary stuff.

4. Re-read your article carefully. (***See also*** "Posting Your First Article," earlier in this part.)

5. After you are done, click Post.

Trumpet spends a few seconds uploading your article to the news server. If you have changed your mind, click Cancel.

Posting a new article

1. View the newsgroup to which you want to post the article. It doesn't matter whether you are viewing an article or not.

2. Click the Post button.

You see the Post Article window. Trumpet fills in the name of the current newsgroup.

3. In the Subject box, enter a subject line. Give the readers enough information to skip the whole article if they wouldn't be interested in your subject. (**See also** "News Netiquette," earlier in this part.)

4. In the Keywords box, type some words that someone may search on to find your article.

5. In the Summary box, you can optionally put a one-line summary of your message.

6. Enter your desired distribution in the Distribution box, or leave it blank for planet-wide coverage. (**See also** Appendix A.)

7. In the large unlabeled box, enter the text of your article.

8. Re-read your article carefully. (**See also** "Posting Your First Article.")

9. After you are done, click Post.

WinSock and MacTCP newsreaders

If you use WinSock or MacTCP software to use the Internet, Trumpet is not the only news reading program you can use. FreeAgent (freeware) and Agent (inexpensive payware) from Forte, Inc., are among the best; find out about them on the Web at `http://www.forteinc.com`. NewsWatcher is popular on the Mac.

Netscape, the famous Web browser, is also an adequate newsreader. If you have version 2.0 or later, choose Window⇨Network News to get started reading news.

Starting Your Own Newsgroup

You can start your own newsgroup, but the process is not for the faint-hearted. Most hierarchies have a `config` newsgroup (for example, `news.config` or `alt.config`), where proposals for new groups are presented, discussed, and disposed of by vote or consensus.

Here are some things you need to do if you want to start a new newsgroup:

✦ Understand Usenet's and your hierarchy's culture.

✦ Read the appropriate `config` group for a while.

✦ Make sure that a suitable group does not already exist.

✦ Pick the right hierarchy and name for your group. `config` groups are really picky about names.

+ Ask for advice in the `config` newsgroup if you are unsure of anything.

+ Write a strong justification for the existence of your new group. How do you know that anyone wants to discuss the topic that you want to start the newsgroup about?

+ Find as many allies as possible.

+ Be tenacious.

Part V

Mailing Lists

A *mailing list* offers a way for a group of people with a shared interest to send messages to each other and hold a group conversation. Mailing lists differ from newsgroups in that a separate copy of the mailing list message is e-mailed to each recipient on the list.

Mailing lists are generally smaller than newsgroups. They can be very specific and tend to be less raucous.

A mailing list has its own mail address; on most lists, anything sent to that address is re-mailed to all the people on the list. People on the list often respond to messages, creating a running conversation. Some lists are *moderated*, which means that a reviewer (moderator) scans messages and decides which to send out.

Remember: Because mailing list messages come via e-mail and all transactions use e-mail, you can participate regardless of what kind of provider you have, just so long as you can send and receive e-mail.

In this part...

- ✔ **Addresses used with mailing lists**
- ✔ **Finding a mailing list**
- ✔ **Getting on and off a mailing list**
- ✔ **Open and closed mailing lists**
- ✔ **Receiving mailing list messages**
- ✔ **Sending messages to a mailing list**
- ✔ **Sending special requests to a mailing list**
- ✔ **Starting your own mailing list**

Addresses Used with Mailing Lists

Every mailing list has *two* mail addresses:

+ **The *list* address:** Messages sent to this address are forwarded to all the people who subscribe to the list.

   Do not use the list address for administrative matters, such as unsubscribing from the list.

+ **The *administrative* address:** Messages sent to this address are read only by the list manager. Use this address for messages about subscribing and unsubscribing.

   Messages to the administrative address are often processed entirely by a computer. In that case, you need to put them in the very rigid formats described in the following sections.

To subscribe to a mailing list, you need its administrative address:

+ **For lists maintained manually:** Add **-request** to the list address. For example, if a manual list is named `unicycles@blivet.com`, the administrative address is almost certainly `unicycles-request@blivet.com`.

+ **For lists maintained automatically:** The request address is usually the name of the type of mail server program at the host where the list is maintained. Look for one of the following server names in a message header to determine how a list is maintained. Common mail server types include:

   • Listproc

   • LISTSERV

   • Mailbase

   • Mailserve

   • Majordomo

For example, the address for a list maintained automatically might look like these:

+ `LISTSERV@blivet.com`

+ `majordomo@blivet.com`

Some list servers do not care if your administrative request is in upper- or lowercase, and others may. In this section, we show all commands in uppercase, which generally works with all servers.

Finding a Mailing List

Stephanie da Silva maintains and updates monthly a large directory of publicly available mailing lists. It's the most complete list of lists we know.

da Silva posts her lists monthly to the Usenet group `news.lists`. The list is also available at `http://www.neosoft.com/internet/paml`.

`http://www.tile.net` has a complete listing of all LISTSERV discussion groups.

Most mail servers will mail you a listing of the mailing lists they support if you send them an e-mail message with the word *LIST* as the body of the message.

Almost any LISTSERV server can search all known LISTSERVs for a mailing list containing a keyword. Send that server e-mail with the message

`LISTS GLOBAL /keyword`

The *keyword* is a word to look for in list descriptions and names. If you leave off the keyword, you get a complete list of LISTSERV lists in your mailbox, which comprises about 700K of text. (Check with your provider to make sure that it can handle that much mail.)

Getting On and Off a Mailing List

The way you get on or off a mailing list — otherwise known as *subscribing* and *unsubscribing* — depends on how the list is maintained.

Lists maintained manually

Send a mail message (like "Please add me to the unicycles list" or "Please remove me from the unicycles list") to the request address.

+ The messages are read by humans, so no fixed form is required.

+ Be sure to include your real name and be polite.

Lists maintained automatically

To join a list, send e-mail to its administrative address with no subject and the following line as the body of the message:

`SUBSCRIBE `*listname your first name your last name*

You don't need to include your e-mail address because it is automatically included as your message's return address. For example, William Clinton would type the following to subscribe to the `leader support` mailing list:

```
SUBSCRIBE leader support William Clinton
```

✦ For Mailbase lists, replace SUBSCRIBE with JOIN.

✦ For Majordomo lists, *don't* include your name.

To get off a list, send e-mail to its administrative address with no subject and the following line as the body of the message:

```
UNSUBSCRIBE listname
```

For Mailbase lists, replace UNSUBSCRIBE with LEAVE.

When subscribing to a list, be sure to send your message from the computer to which you want list messages mailed. Remember, the administrator of the list uses your message's return address as the address he or she adds to the mailing list.

When you first subscribe to a list, you generally receive a welcome message via e-mail. You may want to keep a file of these messages, as they tell what type of server is being used and how to unsubscribe.

Remember: Be sure to send requests to get on and off the list to the administrative address, not to the list itself.

Open and Closed Mailing Lists

Most mailing lists are *open,* meaning that anyone can send a message to the list. Some lists, however, are *closed* and accept messages only from subscribers. Other lists accept members by invitation only.

If you belong to a closed list and your e-mail address changes, you have to let the list maintainers know so that they can update their database.

Receiving Mailing List Messages

As soon as you join a list, you automatically receive all messages from the list along with the rest of your mail.

Some lists are available in *digest* form with all the day's messages combined in a table of contents. To get the digest form, send an e-mail message to the list's administrative address with no subject and the following line(s) as the body of the message:

Server	Message
Listproc servers	SET *listname* MAIL DIGEST
LISTSERV servers	SET *listname* DIGEST
Majordomo servers	SUBSCRIBE *listname* DIGEST UNSUBSCRIBE *listname*

To undo the digest request, send the following message:

Server	Message
Listproc servers	SET *listname* MAIL ACK
LISTSERV servers	SET *listname* MAIL
Majordomo servers	UNSUBSCRIBE *listname* DIGEST SUBSCRIBE *listname*

Sending Messages to a Mailing List

To send a message to a mailing list, just e-mail it to the list's address. The message is automatically distributed to the list's members.

Some lists are *moderated* — in other words, a human being screens messages before sending them out to everybody else, which can delay messages by up to a day or two.

Mail servers usually send you copies of your own messages to confirm that they were received.

You can tell LISTSERV and Listproc not to send you copies of your own messages (or *acknowledge* you) by sending the following message to the administrative address:

Server	Message
Listproc servers	SET *listname* MAIL NOACK
LISTSERV servers	SET *listname* NOACK

To resume receiving copies of your own messages, send this message:

Server	Message
Listproc servers	SET *listname* MAIL ACK
LISTSERV servers	SET *listname* ACK

Sending Special Requests to Mailing Lists

Many mailing lists store their messages for future reference. To find out where these archives are kept, send the following message to the administrative address:

INDEX *listname*

To get a list of (almost) all the people who subscribe to a list, send the following message to the administrative address:

Listproc servers	RECIPIENTS *listname*
LISTSERV servers	REVIEW *listname* BY NAME F=MAIL
Mailbase servers	REVIEW *listname*
Mailserve servers	SEND/LIST *listname*
Majordomo servers	WHO *listname*

Listproc and LISTSERV mail servers won't give your name out by the preceding process if you send the following message to the administrative address:

Listproc servers	SET *listname* CONCEAL
LISTSERV servers	SET *listname* CONCEAL

To unconceal yourself:

Listproc servers	SET *listname* CONCEAL NO
LISTSERV servers	SET *listname* NOCONCEAL

Listservers can do many more tricks. For a list of those tricks, send an e-mail message to LISTSERV@UBVM.cc.buffalo.edu with the following as its body:

GET MAILSER CMD NETTRAIN F=MAIL

Starting Your Own Mailing List

You can start a simple manual list with nothing more than an e-mail program that supports distribution lists. When a message comes in, just forward it to the distribution list.

Before you start a new list, check to see if a list that meets your needs already exists.

You will soon tire of administering your list manually. Many local Internet providers offer mailing list support, sometimes for a small fee. Many universities also maintain mailing lists. If someone in your group has a university affiliation, that person may be able to have a list maintained there.

To add your list to Stephanie da Silva's compilation (*See* "Finding Lists," earlier in this part), send a request to:

`arielle@tarongo.com`.

Include the following information in your request:

◆ The listname

◆ The contact (request) address

◆ The list address

◆ A brief description of your list, following the format of other entries in da Silva's database

Part VI

The World Wide Web

The World Wide Web (WWW, or just Web) is a system linking together many kinds of information all over the world. It is the future of the Internet.

In this part...

- ✔ **Getting started with the Web**
- ✔ **Navigating around the Web**
- ✔ **Understanding Uniform Resource Locators (URLs)**
- ✔ **Using America Online to browse the Web**
- ✔ **Using Lynx to browse the Web**
- ✔ **Using Netscape Navigator to browse the Web**

Getting Started

To start using the World Wide Web, all you need is an Internet connection and a program called a *Web browser* that is compatible with your Internet connection. A Web browser can display the various types of information found on the Web and navigate the connections — called *hypertext links* — built into Web documents.

Understanding some basic concepts is important:

✦ **Hypertext:** Documents that contain pointers, or *hypertext links,* to other documents. Hypertext links appear in a distinct color or are highlighted. When you click a hypertext link, your Web browser displays the document that the link points to, if it's available.

✦ **Uniform Resource Locator (URL):** A single, standard way to write links to the different kinds of information on the Internet. *See* "Uniform Resource Locators (URLs)," in this part.

Common Web browsers and the computer systems for which they are available include:

✦ **Mosaic:** A browser developed by the U.S. National Center for Supercomputer Applications (NCSA), located at `ftp.ncsa.uiuc.edu`. Available for free in versions for Macintosh, Microsoft Windows, and UNIX X Windows. You can get commercial versions from CompuServe and other vendors.

✦ **Netscape Navigator:** A graphical browser developed by Netscape Incorporated, located at `ftp.netscape.com`. Available in versions for Macintosh, Microsoft Windows, and UNIX. A free version is available for students and non-profit use.

✦ **Lynx:** A browser available on UNIX systems and from Internet providers with UNIX shell accounts. Lynx displays only the text portion of Web documents.

✦ **America Online (AOL), eWorld, Prodigy, and The Microsoft Network:** These commercial online services have their own browsers. *See The Internet For Dummies*, 3rd Edition, by John Levine and Carol Baroudi, for details on how to use these services and install their Web browsers. These browsers are similar to, but not the same as, the Netscape Navigator browser described in this part.

✦ **CompuServe:** Provides Web access via PPP connections to your CompuServe account. (See "Protocols" in Part II.) CompuServe lets you download Spry Mosaic for Web browsing. Spry Mosaic is a lot like Netscape Navigator, which is described in this part.

Navigating Around

The Web displays pages of information, with *hypertext links* to other pages.

Browsers display the links differently by highlighting the linked items. Some use a different color for the item, some underline the item, some do both, and some put a code (such as a number in brackets) next to the item.

You can follow these links to see other information:

✦ On a windowed, full-screen system such as Mosaic or Netscape Navigator, use the mouse to click on the link. If the page doesn't fit on the screen, use the scroll bar to scroll up and down.

✦ On a text system that highlights the links, move the cursor to the desired link with the up and down arrow keys and then press Enter.

✦ On a text system that displays links as numbers in brackets, type the number and press Enter. If the page doesn't fit on the screen, press the spacebar or + to go forward a full screen or - to go back.

The Web can handle items other than text pages with links:

✦ Query items let you type in words to search for, and the Web creates a page based on the results of the search.

✦ File items can contain text, pictures, or sound. If your Web browser program can handle the file, it displays or plays it. If not, it just tells you about it.

The Web can handle Gopher, Archie, and WAIS databases. If you have a good Web browser program such as Netscape Navigator or Mosaic, you may find that it is the easiest way to access all these systems. Archie, Gopher, and WAIS are described in Part VIII.

Uniform Resource Locators (URLs)

One of the key advances that Web technology brought to the Internet is the concept of a Uniform Resource Locator (URL). URLs provide a single, standardized way of describing almost any type of information that is available in cyberspace. The URL tells you what kind of information it is (such as a Web page or a Gopher menu), what computer it's stored on, and where on the computer it's located.

URLs are typically long text strings that consist of three parts:

+ Document access type followed by a colon and two slashes (://)

+ Host name of the computer that the information is stored on

+ File path of the file that contains the information

For example:

```
http://world.std.com/~reinhold/papers.html
```

Here, `http` indicates a hypertext document (that is, a Web page). `world.std.com` is the host computer on which the Web page is stored. `/~reinhold/papers.html` is the path and name of a file containing a hypertext index to Arnold Reinhold's online papers.

Common document access types include

+ http:, for hypertext

+ ftp, for File Transfer Protocol

+ gopher:, for gopher

Be careful to enter URLs exactly as they are written, including matching uppercase and lowercase. Most Internet host computers run UNIX, where capitalization counts in directory names and filenames. Copy and paste URLs or bookmarks wherever you can.

Using AOL to Browse the Web

To start the America Online Web browser, choose Internet Connection from the main menu and then click the World Wide Web icon. You see the AOL Web browser window.

When you first start the AOL browser, it goes to a home page. Initially, this is AOL's own home page. You can change the home page location.

1. On the Mac, choose Edit⇔Configure. Under Windows, choose Members⇔Set Preferences. You see the Preferences window.

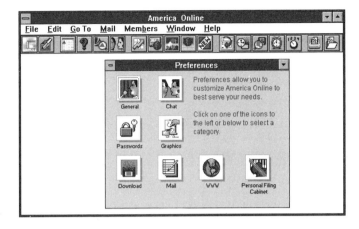

2. Click the WWW icon.

3. Type the URL of the home page you want AOL to start with.

4. Click OK and close the Preferences window.

Following a hypertext link

Hypertext links in the text appear in a distinctive color. Icons or pictures can also be links. They are typically boxed to distinguish them.

Click any link you want to follow. The AOL browser finds and loads the document that the link points to.

✦ AOL tells you how things are going in the upper-left corner of its window. You may have to wait a while.

✦ If you want to give up waiting, click the Stop icon.

Things go a lot faster if you turn off automatic image loading:

1. On the Mac choose Edit⇨Configure. Under Windows, choose Members ⇨Set Preferences. You see the Preferences window.

2. Click the WWW icon.

3. On the Mac, uncheck the Download images box. Under Windows, select No Graphics.

4. Click OK and close the Preferences window. Now when you display a Web page, an icon appears wherever an image should be. Click the icon to load the image.

You can recheck the Download images box in the Edit⇨Configure Preferences dialog box whenever you want.

When you follow a link, the AOL browser changes the link's color. This feature is handy when you are exploring a complex page.

These "followed links" expire after a time, and the color returns to that of an unexplored link. You can control this feature by choosing Edit⇨Configure (Macs) or Members ⇨ Set Preferences (Windows) and clicking the WWW icon.

Going to a URL

Under Windows:

1. Choose Go To⇨Keyword or press Ctrl+K. You see the Keyword window.

2. Carefully type the URL and click Go.

On the Mac:

1. Choose Services⇨Open URL.

2. Carefully type the URL you want and click OK.

You can also type the URL you want into the Current URL text box or use cut and paste to copy it in from another window and press Enter.

You may have to wait a while. AOL tells you how things are going in the upper-left corner of its window.

If you want to give up, click the Stop icon.

Using bookmarks (AOL calls them Hot Lists)

Typing URLs is a pain. When you find a site you like, you can add it to your hot list:

Under Windows:

1. Click the little heart button on the upper-right corner of the window. Or choose Window ⇨Add to Favorite Places.

2. When AOL asks if you want to add it to your hot list, click Yes.

3. To go to a Web page on your hot list, click the Hot List icon on the toolbar (the heart in a folder).

On the Mac:

1. Choose Services⇨Add To Main Hot List. The site's URL is added to your hot list immediately.

2. To go to a bookmark, select it from the Services⇨Hot List menu.

start to get long and unwieldy. Fortu-
ot list. On the Mac, choose
t to create a new hot list file. Under
s icon on the toolbar (the heart in
rite Places, or press Ctrl + B.

b

UNIX. It doesn't display
lips, but it's great for text.

d prompt.

s:

o to. For example:

```
om/~reinhold/papers.html
```

cument, links are underlined or highlighted in bold
video.

1. Press the up- or down-arrow keys to select a particular link.
   Even if the links are on the same line, you still use up and down
   arrow keys.

2. Press Return or the right arrow key when the link you want is
   highlighted.

   Lynx finds the associated file and displays it on-screen.

Browsing with Lynx

Because Lynx is character-based, it cannot display graphics; however, this makes Lynx a very fast Web browser.

You operate Lynx by typing single-key commands, as described in
the following table.

Keystroke Command	Description
Down arrow	Highlight next link.
Up arrow	Highlight previous link.
Right arrow, Return, or Enter	Go to highlighted link.
Left arrow	Go back to previous link (also exits Help).
+ (or space)	Scroll down to next page.
- (or b)	Scroll up to previous page.
? (or h)	Help, go to help pages.
a	Add the current link to your bookmark file.
c	Send a comment to the document owner.
d	Download the current link.
e	Edit the current file.
g	Go to a user specified URL or file.
i	Show an index of documents.
j	Execute a jump operation.
k	Show a list of key mappings.
m	Return to main screen.
o	Set your options.
p	Print to a file, mail, printers, or other.
q	Quit (Capital 'Q' for quick quit).
/	Search for a string within the current document.
s	Enter a search string for an external search.
n	Go to the next search string.
v	View your bookmark file.
z	Cancel transfer in progress.
Ctrl+H or BkSp	Go to the history page.
=	Show file and link information.
\	Change between normal view and document source.
!	Enter a shell command.
Ctrl+R	Reload current file and refresh the screen.
Ctrl+W	Refresh the screen.
Ctrl+U	Erase input line.
Ctrl+G	Cancel input or transfer.

Using Netscape to Browse the Web

Netscape Navigator is the most powerful Web browser (in our humble opinion). Versions are available for Windows, Macs, and UNIX with X Windows.

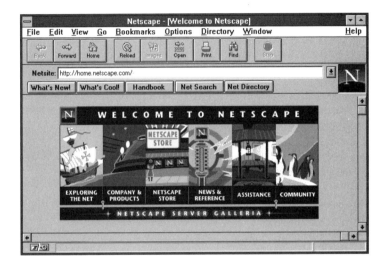

Running Netscape

To run Netscape, double-click its icon (or do whatever you do on your computer to start the program). When you first start Netscape, it goes to a home Web page.

Your starting page is Netscape's own home page. You can change the home page location in the Options⇨General window. Just click the Appearance tab.

Following a hypertext link

Hypertext links in the text appear in a distinctive color. Icons or pictures can also be links and are typically boxed to distinguish them.

Placing the mouse pointer over a link causes the link's URL to appear in the lower-left corner of the Netscape window.

Click any link you want to follow, and Netscape finds and loads the document to which the link points.

✦ Netscape tells you how things are going in the lower-left corner of its window. You may have to wait a while.

✦ If you want to give up, click the Stop icon.

Things will go a lot faster if you turn off automatic image loading:

1. Choose Options from the menu. If a check mark appears to the left of the Auto Load Images item in the Options menu, choose Auto Load Images to turn it off. An icon appears wherever an image should be.

2. Right-click the icon to load that image.

You can reselect the Auto Load Images item in the Options menu whenever you want.

You can ask Netscape to underline links as well. This is handy for black and white screens.

Under Windows:

1. Choose Options ⇨General. You see the Preferences dialog box.

2. Choose the Appearance tab if it's not already selected.

3. In the Link Styles section, click the Underlined box.

4. Click OK.

On the Mac:

1. Choose Options⇨Preferences.

2. Select Windows and Link Styles.

3. Check the Underline Links box.

When you follow a link, Netscape changes its color. This is handy when you are exploring a complex page. These "followed links" expire after a time, and the color returns to that of an unexplored link. You can control this feature in the Options⇨General screen under the Appearance tab.

Going to a URL

1. Click the Open icon or choose File⇨Open Location.

2. Carefully type in the URL and click Open. You may have to wait a while. Netscape tells you how things are going in the lower-left corner of its window.

If you want to give up, click the Stop icon.

You can type the URL directly into the Location or Netsite box at the top of the Netscape screen.

Using bookmarks

Typing URLs is a pain. When you find a site you like, you can add it to your list of bookmarks:

1. Choose Bookmarks⇨Add. The site's URL is added to your bookmark list automatically.

2. To go to a Bookmark, just select it from the Bookmarks menu.

Pretty soon, your bookmark file will start to get long and unwieldy. Fortunately, you can organize your bookmark menu:

1. Choose Bookmarks⇨Go To Bookmarks.

You can drag bookmarks up and down in the list.

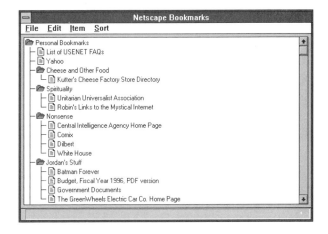

2. Choose Item⇨Insert Separator to put a dividing line in the menu after an item.

3. Choose Item⇨Insert Header and type a name to add a submenu after an item.

4. Click an item and press Delete to get rid of it.

You can also search for a bookmark by using Edit⇨Find.

Part VII

Moving Files with FTP

The Internet allows you to copy files between your computer and other computers on the Internet by using a facility known as FTP (*File Transfer Protocol*). You connect your computer to an *FTP server*, an Internet host computer that stores files for transfer. Many publicly accessible FTP servers allow you to log in and retrieve a wide variety of files, including software, text files, and graphics files.

If your system doesn't handle FTP directly but does have e-mail, you may be able to use e-mail to retrieve files from the Internet. *See* the section "Using FTP via E-Mail," in this part.

In this part...

- ✔ Connecting to a remote system
- ✔ Downloading retrieved files to your PC
- ✔ FTP via mail servers
- ✔ Full-screen FTP programs
- ✔ Leaving FTP
- ✔ Listing the files in directories
- ✔ Moving to other directories
- ✔ Retrieving files and groups of files
- ✔ Storing files on remote systems
- ✔ Uncompressing and decoding retrieved files
- ✔ Using FTP on AOL and CompuServe

Connecting to an FTP Server for Anonymous FTP

On systems that provide files for public download, rather than logging in with your own name, you log in as **anonymous** and use your e-mail address, or the word **guest**, as the password.

Downloading Retrieved Files to Your PC

If you are using a local PC to dial into an Internet shell account, FTP sends files to the Internet provider's computer (host), *not* to your local PC. After the files are on your Internet host, you have to download them to get them to your PC. Exactly how this works depends on the terminal program (communications program) that you use to connect your PC to your Internet shell account.

Downloading details vary but generally resemble the following:

1. Type the command to the host to start the downloading program, such as **sz**, which uses the Zmodem protocol, or **sx**, which uses the Xmodem protocol, followed by the names of the files to download.

2. If your PC terminal program doesn't start downloading automatically, tell it to start downloading (refer to your terminal program's manual).

3. After the files are downloaded and you check that they are okay, delete the copies on the Internet host so that you aren't charged for the disk space.

The Terminal program that comes with Microsoft Windows 3.1 can transfer binary files using either the Xmodem or the Kermit protocol. To transfer a file from a host to your PC:

1. Type the **sx** command to the host to start the downloading program using the Xmodem protocol, followed by the names of the files to download.

2. Choose Settings⇨Binary Transfers and select Xmodem.

3. Choose Transfers⇨Receive Binary File to begin the file transfer.

Using FTP via E-Mail

If your system supports e-mail but not FTP, you can still get limited access to FTP by using a *mail server,* a system that receives e-mail messages and mails back files. Many systems that support anonymous FTP also have mail servers.

For example, rtfm.mit.edu, the system that archives all the periodic Usenet information messages for FTP, also has a mail server with the address mail-server@rtfm.mit.edu.

To find out how to use an FTP-by-mail server, e-mail it a message containing this line:

```
help
```

Typically, you send the system a list of the commands that you *would* have typed to FTP, as in the following:

```
FTP ftp.internic.net
USER anonymous
cd fyi
get fyi-index.txt
quit
```

You can use the following list of public FTP-by-mail servers:

E-Mail Address	Location
bitftp@pucc.princeton.edu	United States
bitftp@vm.gmd.de	Germany
ftpmail@ftp.uni-stuttgart.de	Germany
bitftp@plearn.edu.pl	Poland

The FTP-by-mail system is very popular, and each server has a daily limit on the number of files it will retrieve. This means that it may take as long as a week to answer your request. Don't send another message; that won't help.

Using FTP from a WinSock or MacTCP Program

If you use a SLIP or PPP account, you can use WinSock- or MacTCP-compatible software to communicate with the Internet. Most WinSock and MacTCP programs use a full-screen interface that can display the files in the current directory on your computer and the files in the current directory on the FTP server at the same time. You click buttons to tell FTP what to transfer.

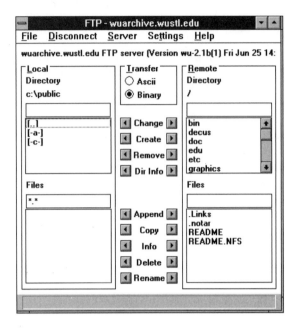

+ To connect to a remote system, choose Connect from the menu. (Once you're connected, the item usually changes to Disconnect, as shown in the figure.)

+ The left side of the window displays information about your own (local) computer. The right side of the window displays information about the FTP server.

+ To change to a different local or remote directory, click the desired directory and then click the appropriate Change arrow.

+ To copy a file, click the file to copy and then click the appropriate Copy arrow.

+ To switch between ASCII (text file) and Binary (non-text file) copying, click the ASCII or Binary button in the Transfer box.

+ After you're done, exit the FTP program the same way you leave any other program on your system; in Windows, for example, choose File⇨Exit or double-click the upper-left corner of the window.

Underneath, the spiffy, windowed programs actually run the same commands as the command line FTP programs. Windowed FTP programs can take a while to start up because they run `dir` commands to get the file lists for the selection windows.

Leaving FTP

When you're done copying files, disconnect from the FTP server.

Using the UNIX FTP program

Type **quit**. FTP exits, as follows:

```
ftp> quit
221 Goodbye
```

Using a graphics FTP program

Click the Disconnect button or choose Disconnect from the menu.

See the section "Using FTP from a WinSock or MacTCP Program," earlier in this part.

Listing the Files in Directories

You can ask your FTP program to display a list of files in the current directory of the FTP server.

Using the UNIX FTP program

Type **dir**.

You see lots of messages, including a list of the files and subdirectories in the current directory. For example:

```
ftp> dir
200 PORT command successful.
150 Opening ASCII mode data connection for /bin/ls.
total 23
drwxrwxr-x 19 root  archive  512 Jun 24 12:09 doc
drwxrwxr-x 5 root   archive  512 May 18 08:14 edu
drwxr-xr-x 31 root  wheel    512 Jul 12 10:37 systems
drwxr-xr-x 3 root   archive  512 Jun 25 1992 vendorware
... lots of other stuff ...
226 Transfer complete.
1341 bytes received in 0.77 seconds (1.7 Kbytes/s)
```

If the directory is so big that it doesn't fit on-screen, you can ask to see just part of it by using *wildcards.* For example, typing **dir c*** asks for just the files starting with the letter *c.*

If you want to store the directory listing on your own computer, you can enter the name of a local file in which you want to store the listing. Use the dir command followed by a . (period), followed by the filename in which to store the result, like this:

```
ftp> dir . file-list
200 PORT command successful.
```

```
150 Opening ASCII mode data connection for /bin/ls.
226 Transfer complete.
45341 bytes received in 42 seconds (1.0 Kbytes/s)
```

If you see a file called README and want to see what's in it before downloading, try this:

```
get README "|more"
```

Using a graphics FTP program

The program displays the list of files automagically. Nice!

Moving to Other Directories

Before you can download a file from the FTP server, you must move to the directory that contains it on the FTP server.

Using the UNIX FTP program

1. Type **cd** followed by the name of the directory you want to change to, like this:

```
ftp> cd edu
250 CWD command successful.
```

2. Type **dir** to see what's in the new directory.

On many systems, all the interesting stuff is stored in a directory called pub. If you don't know where a file is stored, look there first.

Using a graphics FTP program

Click the name of the directory that you want to move to on the Remote (right) side of the FTP window. If you want to move to the parent directory of the current directory, click the .. entry on the directory list.

Retrieving Files

First, you set up to retrieve the files, and then you retrieve them.

Using the UNIX FTP program

1. Use the cd command to move to the directory on the remote computer that contains the files you want. For example:

```
ftp> cd /pub/diaries/packwood
```

2. If the files are not plain text, type **image** or **binary** to tell FTP to transfer the files as binary images, not text files, as in the following:

```
ftp> image
200 Type set to I.
```

3. Type **get**, followed by the filename on the remote computer. If you want to use a different filename on your computer, then put it after the remote filename. For example:

```
ftp> get intro.txt info-file
local: info-file remote: intro.txt
200 PORT command successful.
150 Opening ASCII mode data connection for
  intro.txt (5243 bytes).
226 Transfer complete.
5359 bytes received in 0 seconds (5.2 Kbytes/s)
```

FTP retrieves the file and displays a message about it.

Remember: It can take FTP a long time to retrieve a large file. Allow one second for every 1,000 characters in the file.

If you retrieve a nontext file and it arrives unusable, 95 percent of the time the problem is that you forgot to set the image mode before you retrieved it.

If you change your mind part-way through retrieving a file (for example, you realize that you forgot to type **image** first), interrupt the transfer by typing your interrupt character, usually Ctrl+C or Delete, etc. In windowing systems, click the Cancel button. Interrupting the retrieval process can take 30 seconds or so.

Using a graphics FTP program

Click the names of the files you want to retrieve and then click the arrow button that points from the Remote (right) side of the window to the Local (left) side.

Retrieving Groups of Files (UNIX Only)

To copy a group of files from the same directory, use the `mget` (for *Multiple Get*) command:

1. Move to the directory that contains the files by using the `cd` command.

2. If appropriate, set the image mode by typing **image**.

3. Type **mget** followed by the names of the files you want to get.

You can also use filename patterns that match multiple filenames. The most commonly used pattern is * (which means all files in the directory).

mget asks you about each file that matches the names and patterns in the list.

4. Press y to transfer the file or n to skip it.

Type **prompt** before running mget to turn off the prompting for each file so that mget transfers all the files in the group without asking. Type **prompt** again to turn prompting back on.

Storing Files on FTP Servers

If you have permission, you can store files to the remote system as well. Most anonymous FTP sites will not allow you to do this, though.

Using the UNIX FTP program

1. Type **cd** followed by the directory name on the remote computer where you want to store the file.

2. If the files contain binary data, set the image mode.

3. Type **put**, followed by the name of the file on your computer. If you want to use a different filename on the remote computer, put it after the local filename. For example:

```
ftp> put nigel nigel-data
local: nigel remote: nigel-data
200 PORT command successful.
150 Opening ASCII mode data connection for
  nigel-data.
226 Transfer complete.
795 bytes sent in 0 seconds (0.78 Kbytes/s)
```

You can copy a *group* of files to the remote computer by using the mput command (which stands for *Multiple Put*).

1. Type **mput**, followed by the name of the files to store or a pattern that matches the name of the files to store. The pattern * means all files in the local directory.

As it copies files, mput asks you about each file.

2. Press y to store a file or n to skip it.

To store a group of files without FTP asking you about each one, type **prompt** to turn off name prompting.

Using a graphics FTP program

Click the names of the files you want to send and then click the arrow button that points from the Local (left) side of the window to the Remote (right) side.

Summary of UNIX FTP Commands

Command	Description
get *old new*	Copy remote file *old* to local file *new*. You can omit *new* if it's the same name as *old*.
put *old new*	Copy local file *old* to remote file *new*. You can omit *new* if it's the same name as *old*.
del *xyz*	Delete file *xyz* on the remote system.
cd *newdir*	Change to directory *newdir* on the remote machine.
cdup	Change to next higher directory (the parent directory).
lcd *newdir*	Change to directory *newdir* on the local machine.
asc	Transfer files in ASCII mode (use for text files).
bin or image	Transfer files in binary or image mode (all other files).
quit	Leave FTP.
dir *pat*	List files whose names match pattern *pat*. If you omit *pat*, list all files.
mget *pat*	Get files whose names match pattern *pat*.
mput *pat*	Put files whose names match pattern *pat*.
mdel *pat*	Delete remote files whose names match pattern *pat*.

Uncompressing and Decoding Retrieved Files

After you download a file, you may still have to do some more work before you can use it:

✦ Files on anonymous FTP systems are usually stored in *compressed* format — stored in one of several special formats that squeeze the file into less space.

✦ Often files are *archived* as well, meaning that a group of files is strung together as one file.

✦ Some files are pictures or images that require particular programs to display them.

Remember: The filename *extension* (the part after the dot) tells you how the file is coded and (more important) which program to use to decode it.

Many compression and uncompression programs can be FTPed from `oak.oakland.edu` or `wuarchive.wustl.edu` in the directories `simtel/win3/archiver` and `simtel/msdos/archiver`.

There are far too many ways to store data in files. The following table lists the main categories of files found on FTP servers.

File Type	Description
Archived	Many files combined into one (most archived files are also compressed)
Compressed	A coded form that saves space, with many variants
Images	Digitized pictures in GIF, JPEG, or other image formats
Text	Plain text that can be printed, displayed, and edited with the usual printing and text-editing programs
Uuencoded	Special format that disguises a nontext file as text so that it can be e-mailed

The most common extensions are described in the following sections.

.cpio

Files with the extension .cpio (lowercase) are the products of cpio (CoPy In and Out), a UNIX program with its own format.

To decode the file `blurfle.cpio` on a UNIX system, type
cpio -itcv < blurfle.cpio.

Compressed cpio is also common. Uncompress the file (using gunzip, for example) and then uncpio.

.dd

This is the Macintosh DiskDoubler format. You can get the DD Expand program at no charge.

.hqx

This is the Macintosh Binhex format. Binhex 4.0, which is available as freeware or in Raymond Lau's StuffIt program, will handle this format.

.gif

CompuServe GIF (Graphics Interchange Format) is a popular image format. Most image display programs, such as Netscape Navigator, display GIF files directly. Lview is a widely used GIF viewer for Windows.

.gz and .z

Files with the extensions gz and z (lowercase) are created by the gzip program from the Free Software Foundation's GNU project, which is creating versions of many UNIX utility programs. They are uncompressed by GNU gunzip or Windows WINZIP.

gzip and gunzip are available via FTP from `ftp.uu.net` and `prep.ai.mit.edu`.

GNU gunzip knows about a lot of compression formats and can decompress many other compressed formats.

JPEG

JPEG (Joint Photographic Experts Group) is a popular compressed image format. Most image display programs display JPEG files directly. JPEG images often have the extensions .JPG or .JIF.

.sit

This is a Macintosh StuffIt archive. You can get UnStuffIt as freeware.

.tar

Files with the extension .tar (lowercase) are the products of tar (Tape ARchive), a UNIX archiving program. To unpack a tar file on a UNIX system, type **tar xvf blurfle.tar**.

tar files are also commonly compressed and have names like `blurfle.tar.Z`. Uncompress them and *then* unpack. On some systems these files are called `TAZ` files. Windows WINZIP can unscramble them, too.

.Z

Files with the extension Z (uppercase) are compressed files created by the UNIX compress program. They are decoded with the UNIX program uncompress or Windows WINZIP.

ZIP

Files with the extension ZIP are compressed archives created by the shareware program PKZIP or free ZIP utilities, that can be *unpacked* with the shareware program PKUNZIP, the free program UNZIP, or Windows shareware WINZIP, all widely available.

Compress, gzip, and gunzip are available on `ftp.uu.net` in `/pub/zip`. WINZIP is available on `ftp.winzip.com`.

Using FTP from a UNIX Shell Account

Many FTP programs accept commands that you type. Others, including Netscape, America Online, and CompuServe, display a window with text boxes and buttons. *See* the section "Full-Screen FTP Programs," later in this part.

1. Run the FTP program by typing **ftp** followed by the name of the system to connect to:

```
ftp ntw.org
```

You see a message confirming that you are connected. The program asks for a login name and password.

2. If you have an account on that system, use the same name and password that you use for a direct login, as in the following:

```
Connected to shamu.ntw.org.
220 iecc FTP server (Version 4.1 8/1/91) ready.
Name: elvis
331 Password required for elvis.
Password: type password here
```

On many systems, you can create a file called `.netrc` (or plain `netrc` on non-UNIX systems) that contains the login name for each system that you use often. Each line lists a machine, the login name, and the password for that machine, like this:

```
machine shamu.ntw.org login elvis password sinatra
```

When you FTP to the preceding system, it logs you in automatically.

On some versions of FTP, you can place a default line at the end of the `.netrc`, file that says what login name to use for systems that are *not* listed, as in the following:

```
default login anonymous password elvis@ntw.org
```

Using FTP on America Online

America Online provides FTP access. To use FTP from AOL:

1. Choose Internet Connection from the Main Menu.

2. Click the FTP icon. You see the File Transfer Protocol Window.

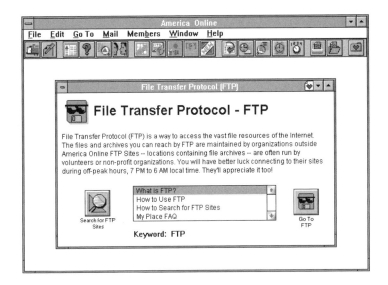

3. Click the Go To FTP icon.

Or you can just enter the keyword FTP.

You see the FTP window with a list of AOL's Favorite FTP servers to choose from. AOL keeps a copy of these sites — *mirrors* them — on AOL's computers so you don't encounter Net delays.

4. Highlight one site and click the Connect button.

If you want a site that is not on the list, click the Other Site button and then type in the site address when asked.

Check the Ask for login Name and Password box if you *don't* want an anonymous FTP connection.

AOL logs in and then shows you the top-level directory at the FTP site you picked. Keep double-clicking folders until you find the file you want; then click Download now.

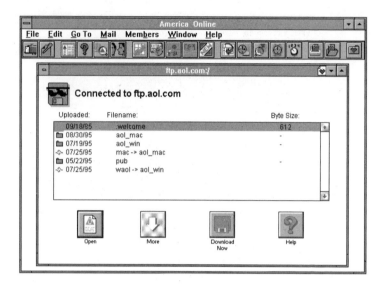

To find an FTP site:

1. Click the Search for FTP Sites icon in the FTP window.

2. Enter a keyword to search for in the thin text box and click the Search button.

You can narrow the search by adding modifiers like AND, OR, and NOT.

A list of matching sites appears in the bigger text box.

3. Double-click a site name to see a description of what's there.

4. If you want to FTP to that site, click the Other Site button in the FTP window and then type in the site address when asked.

You can copy the site name from the top line of the description box and paste it into the Site Address field of the Other Site window.

Using FTP on CompuServe

CompuServe provides FTP access. To use FTP from CompuServe:

1. Click the Internet icon in the Browse menu or Services window, or Go Internet.

2. Click the FTP Icon. The File Transfer Protocol window appears. (You may have to click Proceed to assure CompuServe that you

understand that it's not responsible for files stored on FTP servers.)

3. Click the Access a Specific Site button.

4. Enter Site Name, Directory (if you know it), User Name, and Password.

The User Name and Password fields are filled in properly for anonymous FTP. Just leave them alone if that is what you want.

5. You see an information screen. Just click OK when you are done reading it.

You then see a list of directories and files.

6. Double-click a directory to see its contents.

7. Click a file and then click the Retrieve button to download the file.

To read the contents of a file — for example, a Read file — click the View button.

When you click a file, a box next to its name is checked. You can click several files and then click Retrieve to download all of them.

8. After you're done, click Leave to log off the FTP site.

On the File Transfer Protocol window, you can click the Selected Popular Sites button to see a list of a dozen FTP sites that CompuServe thinks may be of interest.

The Site Description and List of Sites icons display descriptions of popular FTP servers. You can't use these buttons to connect to FTP servers.

Part VIII

Finding Resources on the Net

So many resources are available on the Internet that finding them can be harder than using them.

Archie, Gopher, and WAIS (Wide Area Information Service, pronounced *ways*) are handy systems that keep enormous lists of files on the Internet. These systems also help you find the files you are looking for. The functions of each system overlap, but each has significantly different strengths.

+ If you know the filename that contains the information you want, like a shareware program, use Archie.

+ Gopher is the easiest to use because it's fast, and it presents you with simple menus. It's best for finding text files and interactive services.

+ WAIS is the hardest to use but can do full-text searches in a tremendous number of databases. It's best for finding information that hasn't already been automatically indexed for Gopher or Archie.

In this part...

✔ **Finding files on FTP servers using Archie**

✔ **Finding information in Gopherspace using Gopher**

✔ **Searching text databases using Wide Area Information Service (WAIS)**

Finding Files with Archie

Archie is an Internet service that finds files for anonymous FTP from FTP servers. Archie accepts a keyword or pattern that you enter and looks it up in the database of FTP files kept on an Archie server. For more information about FTP (File Transfer Protocol), *see* Part VII of this book.

You can use Archie in the following ways (each requires that you contact an Archie server):

+ Archie program on a UNIX system

+ E-mail to an Archie server

+ Use a Web page that runs an Archie program

+ Telnet to an Archie server

+ Run a Windows or Macintosh Archie program

Finding public Archie servers

All the Archie servers in the following lists have the same data available. Therefore, you should choose one close to you.

U.S. Public Archie Server	Location
archie.sura.net	Maryland
archie.unl.edu	Nebraska
archie.rutgers.edu	New Jersey
archie.internic.net	New Jersey
archie.ans.net	New York

International Public Archie Server	Location
archie.au	Australia
archie.univie.ac.at	Austria
archie.bunyip.com	Canada
archie.uqam.ca	Canada
archie.funet.fi	Finland
archie.univ-rennes1.fr	France
archie.th-darmstadt.de	Germany
archie.ac.il	Israel
archie.unipi.it	Italy

International Public Archie Server	Location
archie.wide.ad.jp	Japan
archie.sogang.ac.kr	Korea
archie.nz	New Zealand
archie.uninett.no	Norway
archie.icm.edu.pl	Poland
archie.rediris.es	Spain
archie.luth.se	Sweden
archie.switch.ch	Switzerland
archie.ncu.edu.tw	Taiwan
archie.doc.ic.ac.uk	United Kingdom

Requesting information from Archie

Regardless of how you access it (by running a program, using the Web, or sending it e-mail), Archie has four different search modes. How much you know about the name of the file(s) you're looking for determines the search method that you should use. The four different search modes, along with their meanings, follow:

Search Mode	Meaning
sub	Match the search string anywhere in the filename, disregarding capitalization. (This is the mode Archie uses by default.)
subcase	Match the search string exactly as given anywhere in the filename, including matching capitalization.
exact	Search for this exact filename, including matching capitalization. Use this option if possible — it's the fastest.
regex	Use *regular expressions* to define the pattern for Archie's search. (*See* the next section for more information about regular expressions.)

Special characters in Archie regular expressions

A *regular expression* is a formula that tells Archie what types of filenames to find. Archie regular expressions are the same as those used in the UNIX system. See *UNIX For Dummies*, 2nd Edition for more information about regular expressions.

The following is a list of special characters to use in Archie regular expressions, along with what they mean:

Character	Meaning
.	Matches any number of characters.
*	Matches any number of whatever it follows.
[xyz]	Matches any one of the characters in the brackets.
^	Matches the beginning of the name. Inside square brackets, it means to match any character except the ones in the brackets.
$	Matches the end of the name.
\	Causes the next character to be taken literally, not as a special character. To search for U.S.A., for example, type U\.S\.A\.

For example, ^[0-9]*$ matches a name consisting entirely of digits, mac.tcpip matches anything that begins with *mac* and ends with *tcpip*.

The asterisk (*) character does not serve as a wild card the way it does in, say, DOS commands. Use a period (.) instead.

Sending e-mail to Archie

You can use e-mail to communicate with an Archie server. You send information about the file you are looking for, and you receive an e-mail message with a list of the files the Archie server found and where it found them.

1. Send an e-mail message to archie@*server,* where *server* is any of the Archie servers listed in the section "Finding Public Archie Servers," earlier in this part.

2. The Archie server mails back its response.

The following table lists e-mail Archie commands:

Command	Description
prog	Searches for a filename.
whatis	Supplies the keyword for the software description database search.
compress	Sends the reply in a compressed and uuencoded format.
servers	Returns a list of Archie servers.
path	Gives the e-mail address you want Archie to use to respond to your mail request, in case the return address in your mail isn't correct.
help	Returns the help text for e-mail Archie.
quit	Ends the request to Archie.

The most common commands are `prog` and `whatis`. For example, typing the following command searches for files with filenames that start with `font` and end with `.txt`:

```
prog font.*txt
```

TIP

Archie servers are so heavily loaded that it can take several minutes for the Archie server to respond, regardless of how you contact it (*see* the next section). In that case, you may as well mail your request so that you don't have to wait while Archie thinks. Also, for large queries, a large e-mail message is more convenient than seeing the responses fly by in a telnet window.

You can use Web pages to start an Archie search. You fill in the text box in the Web page, click the Search button, and wait for a Web page to appear listing the file the Archie server found.

Here are the URLs of several Web pages:

✦ http://www-ns.rutgers.edu/htbin/archie

✦ http://hoohoo.ncsa.uiuc.edu/archie.html

✦ http://www.thegroup.net/AA.html

✦ http://hoohoo.lerc.nasa.gov/archieplex/

✦ http://www.ucc.ie/cgi-bin/archie

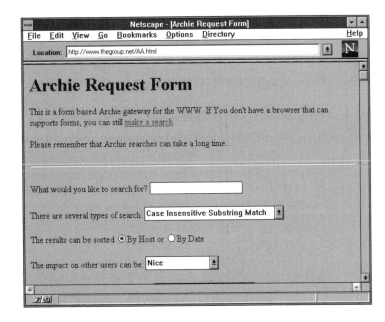

Telnet to connect to Archie

If you don't have an Archie program on your computer (or on your UNIX shell account), you can telnet to Archie — that is, log on to a computer that *does* have an Archie program. Here's how to do it:

1. Telnet to the nearest Archie site. *See* the section "Finding public Archie servers," earlier in this part, for a list of Archie servers, and *see* Part IX for how to use telnet.

See Part IV to learn how to use the `telnet` command.

2. Log in as `archie`, no matter who you actually are.

You get an `archie>` prompt.

3. If you don't want to use the standard sub search (described in the section "Requesting information from Archie," earlier in this part), type this:

```
set search xxx
```

The *xxx* is the type of search you want (sub, subcase, exact, or regex).

4. Type **prog** followed by the string to search for.

For example, to search for filenames that contain *garlic,* type **prog garlic**. Archie returns a list of the matching files.

5. To get a description of a name or term, type **whatis** followed by the name or term.

6. After making as many searches as you want, type **exit** to exit.

7. Use anonymous FTP to retrieve the files. (*See* Part VII.)

Using the UNIX Archie program

If your UNIX system has an Archie program, you can make Archie queries directly:

1. Type **archie** followed by the string to search for, as in

```
archie prune
```

Archie returns a list of the matching files, with directory and host names.

2. Use anonymous FTP to retrieve the files. *See* Part VII.

TIP

Archie usually returns more than one screenful of answers. To view the list one page at a time, use the | character and the `more` command, as in

```
archie garlic | more
```

To save the list in a file, use the > character to redirect the list, like this:

```
archie garlic > garlicfiles
```

You can use the following options to control how the `archie` program works. The following table lists Archie modifiers. Type the option letters after the word *archie*, leaving a space between. For example,

```
archie -elt garlic > garlicfiles
```

Archie Modifier	Equivalent Telnet Command	Meaning
-	`subcase`	Set search mode for a case sensitive substring.
-e	`exact`	Set search mode for an exact string match (default).
-r	`regex`	Set search mode for a regular expression search.
-s	`sub`	Set search for a substring search.
-l		List one match per line.
-t	`sortby`	Sort the output by date, newest first.
-m#	`maxhits`	Set the maximum number of matches to return (default 95).
-h *host*		Specify the Archie server to use.
-L		List the known Archie servers and the current default.

Using the Anarchie program on the Macintosh

Macintosh users can use Anarchie to give a windowed interface to the Archie world.

Finding a file by name

Start by double-clicking the Anarchie application icon. Then follow these steps:

1. Choose File⇨Archie.

2. Select an Archie server from the list.

3. Type the name or part of the name of the file you seek.

4. Click Find.

Anarchie displays a list of matches.

5. Double-click the name of the file you want, and Anarchie downloads the file.

- If the search fails, try another Archie server or search string.

- If the file transfer fails, try another FTP server.

Viewing an FTP server

You can also use Anarchie to download a file without doing an Archie search.

1. Choose File⇨Get.

2. Type the name of the FTP server.

3. Type the path name.

4. Click Fetch.

A list of files and folders appears.

5. Double-click any file or folder to display further lists or to fetch a file.

If you get an error, choose Retry.

Using Gopher to Cruise Gopherspace

Gopher is an Internet search system that lets you navigate through a vast network of Gopher servers, presenting information as a series of menus:

+ Gopher data is physically distributed all over the world, and includes documents, images, and other sorts of data.

+ All the data in the world that is accessible via Gopher is affectionately called *Gopherspace.*

+ Gopher provides a way to find files on systems all over the Net, including information that comes from the finger program (*see* Part IX), Archie (described earlier in this part), telnet (*see* Part IX), and FTP (*see* Part VII).

To use Gopher, you run a Gopher program or some other program that has Gopher capability. Web browsers can access Gopher, as can America Online and CompuServe. UNIX shell accounts usually have the UNIX Gopher program. If all else fails, you can use telnet to connect to a UNIX system that *does* have Gopher.

Using Gopher's menus

All Gopher programs show you a series of menus. Gopher menus can contain the following types of items:

+ Menu items referring to other menus.

+ File items referring to files of text, images, or other data.

+ Search items that let you type in some search text and create a custom menu of items found in the search.

+ Telnet items that start an interactive telnet session to a host that provides a particular service. If you need to log in to the host, Gopher tells you the login name to use.

Some Gopher client programs have limits on the kinds of files they can handle. In particular, the UNIX Gopher program can display files that contain only plain text; however, it can copy any file to your local machine if you want to deal with it later.

Using Gopher on AOL

To use Gopher from America Online:

1. Select Internet Connection from the Main Menu.

2. Click the Gopher & WAIS icon from the Internet Connection window.

Or you can just enter the keyword **gopher**.

You see a list labeled Main Categories.

3. Double-click folders in the list box until you see a file you want.

4. Double-click the file to view it.

5. Choose File⇨Save to save the information in the file on your computer.

To search Gopherspace on AOL by using Veronica:

1. Click the Search All Gophers icon in the Gopher & WAIS window.

2. Enter your search keywords in the thin text box, using **AND**, **OR**, and **NOT** as appropriate.

3. Click the Search button.

Using Gopher on CompuServe

To access Gopher from CompuServe, telnet to one of the public Gopher servers listed under "Finding Gopher programs," later in this part.

Telnet from CompuServe is described in Part IX.

Using Gopher from the Web

Gopher sites are part of the World Wide Web, too. Just point your Web browser to this URL, gopher:⫫gopherserver-address, where *gopherserver-address* is the Internet address of the server. *See* Part VI for more information on the Web.

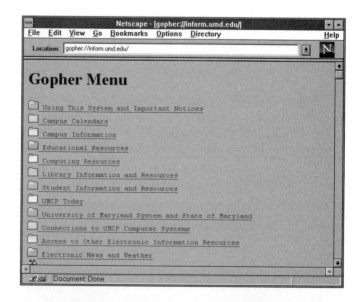

Using HGopher under MS Windows

HGopher is a graphical user interface for Gopher that runs under Microsoft Windows.

To use it, follow these steps:

1. In Program Manager, double-click the HGopher icon.

HGopher displays a screen like this:

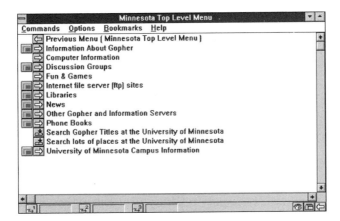

The column of icons describe the file type:

- The eyeglasses mean a text file.

- Arrows are menus.

- A little arrow pointing at a book is a search item.

- The 1101 is a binary file.

- Telnet items (none shown here) appear as little terminals.

2. To select an item, click its icon. If there is a second icon to the left of the item, click that icon to find out some extra information describing the item.

When you select a search item, HGopher pops up a window into which you type search terms.

When you select a file item, HGopher starts up a suitable program to view that item (such as Windows Notepad for a text file).

If you click the eyeball at the lower-right corner of the screen when you have selected a file item, HGopher asks you for a local filename into which to copy the file. This allows you to save files locally. Click the eye again to return to viewing selected files.

When you select a telnet item, HGopher pops up a window telling you the login name to use. When you click OK, it opens a telnet window to the remote system.

HGopher can have up to three files and telnet windows open at one time, and you can continue moving through menus while it is retrieving a file to be displayed.

Using TurboGopher on a Macintosh

TurboGopher is a graphical user interface for Gopher that runs on the Macintosh.

+ Launch the TurboGopher program.

+ TurboGopher goes to its Home Gopher. Choose Gopher➪Select Another Gopher to go elsewhere.

+ Double-click any interesting item to open it.

+ When you double-click a file, TurboGopher fetches and displays that file.

+ Double-click a folder to display its contents.

+ Double-click the Search (question mark) icon to search a database by specifying one or more keywords.

+ Disk icons represent archived Mac software. The freeware application, StuffIt Expander, is recommended for unpacking these files.

+ Items marked PC are for MS-DOS or Microsoft Windows.

+ Items marked UX are for UNIX.

+ Documents with a starburst on them are graphics files in GIF, JPEG, or PICT format. TurboGopher can launch a picture-viewing application, like JPEGView, to let you see the picture.

+ Items with an *h* in the icon are HTML (World Wide Web) files. TurboGopher can pass them to a Web browser like Netscape Navigator.

+ Double-click a terminal icon to launch telnet (or TN3270 if appropriate) and initiate a terminal session to a terminal-based information system like a library catalog.

Finding Gopher servers

Most Internet providers offer a local Gopher program (known as a *Gopher client*) called Gopher. This Gopher program connects to a *Gopher server,* an Internet host computer that actually provides the information.

If your system doesn't have a Gopher program, you can telnet directly to one of the public Gopher servers listed in the following tables, all of which run the original UNIX gopher program. Use the login name listed in the table if you want to use gopher. If no login name is listed, log in as **gopher**.

U.S. Public Gopher Server	Location	Login Name
infoslug.ucsc.edu	California	
pubinfo.ucsd.edu	California	infopath
ux1.cso.uiuc.edu	Illinois	
panda.uiowa.edu	Iowa	
inform.umd.edu	Maryland	
gopher.ora.com	Massachusetts	
consultant.micro.umn.edu	Minnesota	
gopher.msu.edu	Mississippi	
nicol.jvnc.net	New Jersey	NICOL
ecosys.drdr.virginia.edu	Virginia	
gopher.virginia.edu	Virginia	gwis
telnet.wiscinfo.wisc.edu	Wisconsin	wiscinfo

International Public Gopher Server	Location	Login Name
info.anu.edu.au	Australia	info
finfo.tu-graz.ac.at	Austria	info
tolten.puc.cl	Chile	
ecnet.ec	Ecuador	
gopher.torun.edu.pl	Poland	
gopher.uv.es	Spain	
gopher.brad.ac.uk	United Kingdom	info

Using the UNIX Gopher program

If you use a UNIX shell account, run the gopher program.

1. If your system has its own Gopher program, run it by typing **gopher**.

2. If your UNIX system doesn't have the gopher program, telnet to a UNIX system that does. *See* Part IX of this book for how to telnet. Then run the program by typing **gopher**.

You see a menu like this:

```
Internet Gopher Information Client v1.1
Root gopher server: gopher.micro.umn.edu

-> 1. Information About gopher/
   2. Computer Information/
   3. Discussion Groups/
   4. Fun & Games/
   5. Internet file server (ftp) sites/
   6. Libraries/
   7. News/
   8. Other Gopher and Information Servers/
   9. Phone Books/
   10. Search Gopher Titles at the University of
   Minnesota <?>
   11. Search lots of places at the University of
   Minnesota <?>
   12. University of Minnesota Campus Information/
   Press ? for Help, q to Quit,u to go up a menu
   Page: 1/1
```

3. To move to a particular item, use the up- and down-arrow keys or type the line number of the item. Items that end with a slash display other menus, items that end with something in < > are search or telnet items *(see* "Using Gopher to telnet," later in this part), and items that end with neither are files.

To select an item, move the cursor to it and press Enter.

4. To exit Gopher, press q. If it asks if you really want to quit, press y.

If the menu is larger than the screen, press + and - (or use the arrow keys) to scroll up and down. To return to the preceding menu, press u. To return to the first menu, press m.

You can copy files that you find with Gopher from your Internet provider's computer to your own computer by using the original UNIX Gopher program.

Note: This works only if you are using a Gopher client program on your own computer, not if you telnet to a Gopher server.

✦ For text files, Gopher shows the file a screen at a time. Press the spacebar to move from screen to screen or press q to stop viewing the file.

✦ Press s to save the file on your own computer.

✦ Press m to send the file to you as e-mail. It asks for your e-mail address. ***See*** Part III of this book for information about e-mail.

Saving files to a PC or Mac

If you dial into a UNIX Gopher program from a PC or Mac using a terminal program (such as Kermit, Crosstalk, ProComm, Zterm, or Microphone), you can download files directly to your system.

1. On the menu in which the file appears, move the cursor to the file item but do not press Enter.

2. Press D (for Download).

Gopher pops up a window listing the download schemes that it can use, with numbers by each one.

3. Type the number that corresponds to a download protocol that your terminal program supports. The most popular protocols are Kermit, Zmodem, or Xmodem.

4. If it doesn't do so automatically, tell your terminal program to start downloading. The information is copied to your disk.

Searching with UNIX Gopher

If you can't find the information you're looking for by moving around the menus (as described in the section "Using the UNIX gopher program," in this part), try *searching:*

1. Run Gopher as described in the section "Using the UNIX Gopher program," in this part.

2. Select a search item by moving to it and pressing Enter.

In Gopher menus, menu items that you can search are indicated by ⟨?⟩.

1. Gopher pops up a box into which you can type search terms. Type a word or a few words that describe what you are looking for and press Enter.

Gopher shows you a menu consisting of the items that matched.

2. Select items on that menu as you would on any other menu.

Gopher has special *CSO* searches for finding people in organizations, letting you type in lots of different facts about the person you're looking for. Often, just typing in the person's first name followed by his or her last name is enough to find someone.

A program called Veronica searches through all available Gopher menus to find items that match your words. It's a quick way to find something whose name you know. To find a Veronica search item, look on the Home Gopher menu, which is usually available on the first menu that Gopher shows you.

Using bookmarks in UNIX Gopher

You can use bookmarks to remember interesting places as you navigate through Gopherspace.

- ✦ To put a bookmark on the current item, press a (lowercase).
- ✦ To put a bookmark on the current menu, press A (uppercase).
- ✦ To see a menu of all your bookmarks, press v.
- ✦ To select an item from that menu, move the cursor to it and press Enter.
- ✦ To delete an item from the bookmark menu, move the cursor to it and press d.

If you telnet to Gopher, the program remembers your bookmarks only until you log out. If you run Gopher on your local computer, the program remembers your bookmarks in a file so they are available any time.

Summary of UNIX Gopher commands

The following table contains basic UNIX Gopher commands:

Command	Meaning
Enter	Select current item, same as right arrow.
u	Up, go back to preceding menu, same as left arrow.
+	Move to next menu page.
−	Move to preceding menu page.
m	Go to main menu.
digit(s)	Go to particular menu item, terminate with Enter.
/	Search menu for string.
n	Search for next match.
q	Quit gopher.
=	Describe current item.

The following table contains UNIX Gopher bookmark commands:

Command	Meaning
a	Add current item to bookmark list.
A	Add current menu to list.
v	View bookmarks as a menu.
d	Delete current bookmark.

The following table contains UNIX Gopher file commands:

Command	Meaning
m	Mail current file to user.
s	Save current file (not for telnet).
p	Print current file (not for telnet).
D	Download current file.

Using Gopher to telnet

If you find something interesting in Gopher and are told that you have to telnet to another system to see it, Gopher offers to do the telnetting for you automatically.

On UNIX Gopher menus, telnet items end with <TEL>. Other Gopher programs mark telnet items with an icon of a computer.

1. Select a telnet item by moving the cursor to it and pressing Enter.

The Gopher program pops up a window that warns you that you are about to telnet to someplace else and gives you the login name to use.

The telnet session starts.

2. Log in when prompted to, using the name supplied.

3. Use the system to find the information you wanted.

4. When you log out, you return to the Gopher program.

If Gopher can telnet to a system, you can telnet there yourself. Note the name of an especially useful system and the required login name and then telnet there directly next time. *See* Part IX of this book for information about telnet.

Searching Text Databases with WAIS

WAIS stands for Wide Area Information Service, an Internet full-text search facility. The basic steps in any WAIS search are:

1. Decide which document sources to search.

2. Enter search words and do the search.

3. Retrieve interesting documents.

4. If needed, do a revised search.

Searching for text

You give WAIS a list of words, and it looks through a big set of documents and finds the ones that best match the search words. Unlike Archie and Gopher, WAIS looks at the *contents* of files, not just at the titles of files.

Some versions of WAIS also feature *relevance feedback*. After WAIS does a search, you can mark a few of the documents that it found as most relevant and then redo the search. WAIS then tries to find more documents similar to the ones that you marked.

✦ If your computer system has a WAIS program, run it.

✦ The easiest way to do a WAIS search is from the Web page at
   http://www.wais.com/.

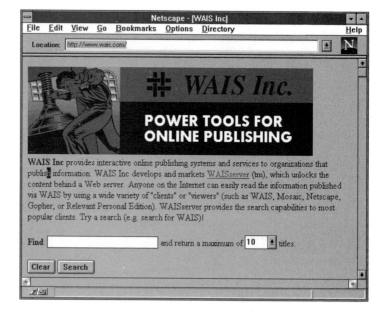

✦ You can also telnet to a computer that has WAIS. **See** Part IX of this book for more on telnet.

✦ We recommend telnetting to wais.com, the home of WAIS. Log in as **wais**.

✦ WAIS starts out showing a single entry, the *directory of servers* (also known as *sources*).

✦ Use WAIS to search for information (**see** other WAIS entries in this part of this book).

◆ When you are done, escape from WAIS by pressing q. Depending on where you are, you may have to press q three or four times to get out of the program.

Searching for text in documents

Note: Before you can search for text within documents, be sure that you have already selected the document sources to search in.

See the WAIS section "Selecting databases to search," later in this part, to learn how to select the document sources.

1. After you have selected the WAIS document sources you want, press Enter to prepare to search.

2. WAIS shows you the current list of keywords. You can press Ctrl+U to clear the list if need be and then add new terms if desired.

3. Press Enter again to perform the search. The result resembles the following figure:

4. Now you can look at the documents that WAIS found. Move the cursor to the desired document with the arrow keys or type the line number followed by Enter.

5. Press the spacebar to retrieve the document.

6. WAIS displays the document a page at a time. Press the spacebar to move from page to page or press q to stop displaying the document.

7. After displaying as many documents as you want, press s to prepare for another search or q to exit.

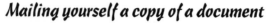

Mailing yourself a copy of a document

To e-mail yourself a copy of a document, type | (vertical bar) followed by **mail *name@host*,** where *name@host* is your e-mail address. Then press Enter. You only have to enter this information once — after that, WAIS remembers the command; so you need only press | and Enter.

See *The Internet For Dummies,* 3rd Edition, Chapter 12.

Selecting databases to search

WAIS can search hundreds of different databases. Here's how to select which databases — also known as *document sources* — to search:

1. Run WAIS.

 You should see a list of hundreds of document sources that WAIS is prepared to search.

 If not, see the next section, "Server database," to find out how to add sources to the list.

2. Navigate through the list:

 • Press the down-arrow key or j (lowercase) to move down the list.

 • Press the up-arrow key or k (lowercase) to move up the list.

 • To move down a page at a time, press J (uppercase).

 • To move up a page at a time, press K (uppercase).

 When you get to the end of the list, WAIS shows you the beginning again. Likewise, when you move up to the beginning, WAIS shows you the end (it's an endless loop).

 You can also move right to a document source on the list by pressing / (slash) followed by the name of the document source.

3. When you see a document source that might contain the information you want, select it by pressing the spacebar or . (period). You can select as many document sources as you want.

 WAIS confirms that you have selected the document source by displaying an asterisk. (Pressing the spacebar for a selected source deselects it.)

4. Now you are ready to tell WAIS what to search for, as described in the WAIS section "Searching for text in documents," earlier in this part.

Server database

If you can't find any promising document sources, select the document source called *Database of Servers* and search it for more possible databases.

Follow these steps:

1. Run WAIS.

2. Select the Database of Servers by moving the cursor to it and pressing the spacebar or . (period).

3. Press w to tell WAIS that you want to enter the text to search for.

4. Enter some words describing the kinds of topics you want.

5. Press Enter to search for document sources. WAIS gives you a chance to add more keywords — do so if you want and then press Enter to start the search.

WAIS finds a list of document sources.

6. Move to an interesting document source with the up- and down-arrow keys or type the line number followed by Enter.

7. Press the spacebar to look at the source description. Press the spacebar to page through the description if it is more than one page.

8. To add the server to the list that WAIS can use, press u.

9. Repeat these steps for as many sources as you want.

10. Press s to return to the WAIS sources screen.

Part IX

Online Communication

Several facilities put you into direct contact with other computers on the Internet.

This part shows you how to check the status of a computer or person, chat with someone else on another computer, and log into other computers on the Net as though you were connected to them directly.

In this part...

✔ finger

✔ talk and ntalk

✔ telnet

✔ tn3270

Finding Public Systems to Telnet to

You can find public systems to which you can telnet in many online ways:

✦ Scott Yanoff publishes a regularly updated online resource guide. `finger yanoff@csd4.csd.uwm.edu` to find out how to get a copy.

✦ The Washington University Libraries in St. Louis, Missouri offer WorldWindow, a gateway to dozens of login services. Telnet to `library.wustl.edu` (no login needed).

✦ `hytelnet` is a system that provides access to libraries around the world. You can access catalogs, online books, and other information. Telnet to `access.usask.ca`, `info.ccit.arizona.edu`, `nctuccca.edu.tw`, `info.mcc.ac.uk`, or `rsl.ox.ac.uk`, and log in as **hytelnet**. Or telnet to `laguna.epcc.edu` or `info.anu.edu.au` and log in as **library**.

Using finger

`finger`, a program supported by many direct Internet providers, lets you ask about the status of a computer or person.

Checking up on other computers

On UNIX systems, type **finger @** (that's an *at* sign) followed by the host computer's name on the command line, like this:

`finger @shamu.ntw.org`

On windowing systems, start the `finger` program and then enter the Internet host name in the appropriate field in the program window.

`finger` returns a list of the people currently using the remote computer. The format varies considerably from one system to another, but the following is a typical list:

Login	Name	TTYIdle	When	Office
root	0000-Admin	co 12:	Wed 16:04	
johnl	John R. Levine	vt 1d	Wed 16:03	Rm 201A
johnl	John R. Levine	p0	Wed 16:10	Rm 201A
johnl	John R. Levine	p1 1	Wed 16:10	Rm 201A

Checking up on other people

You can check up on people using other computers on the Net by using `finger`:

On UNIX systems, type **finger** followed by the user's name, and then @ followed by the host computer's name on the command line, as in

```
finger johnl@dummies.com
```

On windowing systems, start the `finger` program and then enter the user and Internet host names in the appropriate fields in the program window.

The address you need for `finger` is often the same as the person's e-mail address.

The result varies from machine to machine. The following is typical:

```
Login name: johnl    In real life: John R. Levine
Directory: /usr/johnl      Shell: /bin/sh
On since Jun 30 16:03:13 on vt01  9 hours Idle Time
Project: Working on "Internet For Dummies Quick Ref"
Plan: Write many books, become famous.
```

On many systems, you can have information displayed when someone "fingers" you. You can put a one-line summary in the file .project and a longer description (up to ten lines or so) in .plan.

Many organizations, particularly universities, let you use `finger` to look up information like phone numbers and office locations. For example, to find someone at the Massachusetts Institute of Technology, enter

```
finger lastname-firstname@mit.edu
```

Similar servers exist at Yale (@directory.yale.edu), Boston University (@bu.edu), the University of California at San Diego (@ucsd.edu), and other schools. A few companies also have directory servers.

Remember: You can always try to access such a server, since the worst that can happen is that you won't get a useful answer back.

Getting other information

Some systems use `finger` as an easy way to query databases. The available information ranges from the profound to the silly. For example:

+ `finger nasanews@space.mit.edu` for a list of recent NASA press releases

+ `finger copi@oddjob.uchicago.edu` for an almanac of today's birthdays, anniversaries, and sports events

+ `finger quake@geophys.washington.edu` for a list of earthquakes in the past few days

These `finger` commands frequently return more than one screenful of stuff. If you're using a UNIX-based provider, use the `more` command to see the result a page at a time, like this:

`finger someservice@somesite | more`

See *The Internet For Dummies,* 3rd Edition, for more information about `finger`.

Using talk

`talk` lets you chat with, or type back and forth to, someone else on another computer.

Some systems have "old talk" called `talk` and "new talk" called `ntalk`. If your system has both, use `ntalk`.

You cannot use `talk` to chat with users of commercial providers like AOL and CompuServe. They have their own internal chat systems.

Initiating a conversation

To start a `talk` session from a UNIX system, type **talk**, followed by the user's name, **@**, and finally the host computer's name.

You usually can just type

`talk mail-address`

`talk` notifies the other person and displays [Waiting for your party to respond] on your screen.

When the other person responds, `talk` displays [Connection established], at which point you can start typing.

The `talk` commands split the screen in half: What you type appears in the top half, and what the other person types appears in the bottom half.

Refusing talk connections

You can decline to engage in a talk session.

+ To turn off talk requests, type **mesg n** at the command prompt.

+ To turn on talk requests, type **mesg y** at the command prompt.

+ To find out whether you're receiving requests, type **mesg** at the command prompt.

If you try to talk to someone who has turned off talk requests, `talk` displays [`Your party is refusing messages`]. Likewise, if someone else tries to talk to you and you have turned off talk requests, the person sees that same message.

Some commands turn off talk requests while they run (they simply want to keep the screen clear). Therefore, if your request to talk is refused, try again a few minutes later — your request may have been blocked by a program protecting its screens rather than denied by someone who's not feeling chatty.

Responding to someone else's request to talk

When someone else wants to talk to you, your computer displays

```
Message from Talk_Daemon@shamu ...
talk: connection requested by king@NTW.ORG.
talk: respond with:  talk king@NTW.ORG.
```

If you want to talk, type the command that `talk` suggests (in this case, type **talk king@NTW.ORG**).

`talk` splits the screen and reports [`Connection established`].

Start typing.

Stopping a talk session

When you're done with your talk session, hang up by pressing your *interrupt key* (usually Ctrl+C or Del).

`talk` displays [`Connection closed. Exiting`] and breaks the connection.

Remember: Either party can end the talk session.

Using telnet

`telnet` enables you to log into other computers on the Net as if you were connected to them directly.

Don't worry — it's perfectly legal! `telnet` works only if the other computer gives permission.

Connecting to remote computers

On UNIX systems, you type **telnet** followed by the host name of the computer you want to log into.

On windowing systems, you type the host name into a pop-up window. (If you don't see a pop-up window, choose Connect from the menu.)

telnet then connects your computer to the remote system.

In the process of connecting from a UNIX system, telnet tells you the *escape character* — the key combination to press if you have trouble disconnecting from the remote computer. Make a note of it! (If you didn't, try Ctrl+].)

At this point, the remote system usually asks you to enter your user name *on that system* and then your password.

Some systems don't need a login and move directly to a welcome screen.

After telnet makes contact with the remote computer, it may ask you what kind of terminal you're using (common terminal types include VT100, ANSI, and 3101). If you indicate the wrong type, the information on your screen will be scrambled. If telnet suggests a terminal type, accept it and see what happens.

Most systems provide telnet access on the standard telnet port — port number 23. A few systems, though, use a different port to provide direct access to a particular service.

✦ On UNIX systems, type the port number after the system name on the command line. For example, telnet martini.eecs.umich.edu 3000 is a system that looks up place names in the U.S.

✦ On windowing systems, type the port number in the window where you select the system you want to connect to.

Connecting via CompuServe

You can access remote computers from CompuServe by using telnet:

1. Choose Internet from the Browse menu.

2. Click the telnet icon in the Internet window.

3. Double-click Access a Specific Site in the text list.

4. Enter the site name in the pop-up window.

You then see the CompuServe terminal emulator window with the telnet login sequence from the remote computer.

5. Follow the steps under "Connecting to remote computers" to complete your connection.

Disconnecting from remote computers

You end a telnet session by logging out and ending the connection.

Log out from the remote system as if you were connected directly. Usually, you log out by typing **logout**, **exit**, or **bye** or pressing Ctrl+D.

telnet closes the connection and (on most systems) exits.

On windowing systems, if telnet doesn't exit, just close the window. For example, in Microsoft Windows, double-click the box at the window's upper-left corner.

If the remote system is recalcitrant and doesn't log you out, try the following steps.

On UNIX systems:

1. Type the escape character, which is usually Ctrl+] (close square bracket). You should see a prompt like

    telnet>

If you don't get the telnet> prompt in a second or two, press Enter.

2. Type **quit** and press Enter.

    telnet closes the connection and exits.

On windowing systems, simply choose from the menu the item that disconnects the remote system.

Using tn3270 to Connect to IBM Mainframes

Many IBM mainframe computers expect you to use a terminal known as a 3270. The regular telnet program, however, is lousy at pretending to be a 3270. So if you're talking to an IBM mainframe, try using tn3270 rather than telnet; you get snappier responses and better-looking screens.

In addition, unlike regular telnet, tn3270 lets you use cursor keys reliably to move anywhere on-screen. When you finish filling in the blanks, you press Enter to send everything to the remote computer.

If you're not sure whether you've contacted an IBM mainframe computer, remember that IBM mainframes use LOTS OF CAPITAL LETTERS and acronyms such as VM, CMS, and MVS.

Part X

Indispensable Internet Resources

The Internet is too big and changing too quickly for a comprehensive summary in a book this size. This part, however, gives you a list of indispensable Internet resources. They will help you find the other resources you need.

We give URLs for most of the resources — *see* Part VI for what to do with a URL.

In this part...

- ✔ The CIA World Fact Book
- ✔ Infoseek
- ✔ Library of Congress
- ✔ MagicURL Mystery Trip
- ✔ Net-Happenings
- ✔ NEW-LIST
- ✔ news.announce.newusers
- ✔ A Reporter's Internet Survival Guide
- ✔ The Virtual Tourist II
- ✔ Yahoo!

The CIA World Fact Book WWW Pages

`http://www.odci.gov/cia/publications`

The Almanac of the Internet. Here, you can get detailed information about every country in the world, along with digital reference maps and appendices on international organizations.

Infoseek WWW Page

`http://www.infoseek.com`

Infoseek is a powerful Internet searcher. It attempts to index almost everything that's on the Net. Infoseek's basic services are free; they charge for a more advanced package. You type in search words, and Infoseek returns Web pages that best match your request.

Here are some ways to sharpen your Infoseek search request:

✦ Only capitalize words when you're sure that they would be stored that way: for example, proper or place names.

✦ Infoseek treats adjacent capitalized words as a single proper name. To find mentions of Elvis Presley, just enter **Elvis Presley**.

✦ If you need more than one capitalized name, put a comma between them.

   Example: `Bill Clinton, Little Rock`

✦ Don't use words like *and*, *or*, and *not* to condition your search. Infoseek just treats them as additional search words.

✦ Infoseek does not understand wildcard characters like * or ?.

✦ Capitalize common words that are important to your search, such as Next.

✦ Infoseek orders its answers by how good it thinks each match is.

✦ If you don't like the answers you get, check your spelling and remove unneeded capitalization; then try to express your search in different words.

✦ Put "double quotation marks" around words you would expect to see right next to each other.

✦ Put a hyphen (-) between words you would expect to see within one word of each other.

✦ Put [square brackets] around words you expect to appear near each other (within 100 words).

✦ Put a + in front of any word that should appear in every document that Infoseek presents.

✦ Put a - in front of any word that should *not* appear in any document Infoseek finds for you. Make sure that you put a space before the - and none between it and the word.

Examples:

```
repairs "fax machines" +Chicago
"word processors" -Windows -Macintosh
[jobs Massachusetts Internet writer]
```

Library of Congress WWW Page and Telnet Site

http://www.loc.gov/ or telnet to locis.loc.gov

The United States Library of Congress is the world's largest library. In addition to having its card catalog online, the LOC has pointers to a wide variety of Internet resources, both within and outside the United States Government. Here is a sample of the Library of Congress Indexes to Other World Wide Web Services:

✦ U.S. Government: General Resources

✦ U.S. Government: Executive Branch: Information about the White House and U.S. Executive Branch agencies

✦ U.S. Government: Legislative Branch: Information about the U.S. Congress and its support agencies

✦ State and Local Governments: Information about U.S. state and local governments

✦ Library and Information Science Resources

✦ Newspapers, Current Periodicals & Government Documents: Links to online news sources, newspapers, periodicals, and government documents

✦ Electronic Texts and Publishing Resources: Internet resources for electronic texts, online booksellers, and publishing houses

✦ Greek and Latin Classics Internet Resources: Links to major Internet sites featuring Greek and Latin Classics resources as well as sites in specific Classics disciplines such as archaeology, paleography, papyrology, and so on

✦ Internet Resources: Information about Internet Resources: Guides, Tools, Training, Policies, Standards, Access Providers, and Business Services

✦ World Wide Web Meta-Indexes and Search Tools: Indexes of Web servers arranged by subject or geographically, and a collection of tools to search the Web

✦ World Wide Web How-To's: Resources for learning how to build Web servers and HTML documents

MagicURL Mystery Trip WWW Page

`http://www.netcreations.com/magicurl/`

You want to show off the Internet, but you're tired of the same old, same old. This award-winning site will take you somewhere at random from a large list of sites that Ryan Scott has screened for cool.

Net-Happenings WWW Page and Mailing List

`http://www.mid.net/NET/`

Gleason Sackman's daily list is one of the best ways to keep up with what's happening on the Internet. You can inspect it at this Web site or subscribe to the digest as a mailing list:

Administrative address: `majordomo@dsmail.internic.net`

Commands:

✦ `subscribe net-happenings`

✦ `unsubscribe net-happenings`

✦ `info net-happenings`

Address for submitting announcements:

`net-happenings@dsmail.internic.net`

NEW-LIST Mailing List

NEW-LIST tells you about new mailing lists when they start up. It's a great way to get a sense of the Internet ground-game.

To subscribe, send e-mail to

`listserve@vm1.nodak.edu`

with the message body

`SUBSCRIBE NEW-LIST` *yourname*

news.announce.newusers Newsgroup

The Usenet newsgroup news.announce.newusers has well-chosen articles of interest to new and veteran Internet users. Articles are re-posted regularly. Here is a typical sample:

+ Anonymous FTP: Frequently Asked Questions (FAQ) List

+ FAQ: How to find people's E-mail addresses

+ How to become a Usenet site

+ How to find the right place to post (FAQ)

+ How to Create a New Usenet Newsgroup

+ Introduction to the *.answers newsgroups

+ Advertising on Usenet: How To Do It, How Not To Do It

+ Copyright Myths FAQ: 10 big myths about copyright explained

+ Emily Postnews Answers Your Questions on Netiquette

+ A Primer on How to Work With the Usenet Community

+ Introduction to news.announce

+ Guidelines on Usenet Newsgroup Names

+ How to Get Information about Networks

+ Usenet Software: History and Sources

+ Answers to Frequently Asked Questions about Usenet

+ Rules for posting to Usenet

+ A Guide to Social Newsgroups and Mailing Lists

+ Hints on writing style for Usenet

+ What is Usenet?

+ What is Usenet? A second opinion.

+ FAQs about FAQs

A Reporter's Internet Survival Guide WWW Page

http://www.qns.com/~casey/

This is a good compendium of Internet resources for anyone looking for hard information. It was developed by Patrick Casey of the Associated Press.

The Virtual Tourist II WWW Page

`http://wings.buffalo.edu/world/vt2/`

This page is a starting point for finding information about localities in the United States and throughout the world. It includes general information, tourist guides, and pictures for thousands of places.

Organized as a series of maps, it starts with a map of the entire planet. Point and click until you get where you want to go.

Yahoo! WWW Page

`http://www.yahoo.com`

Yahoo is an excellent outline index to the Internet. Using Yahoo is like spending an afternoon wandering around in a library.

Yahoo has a search facility, but it is less powerful than Infoseek's. Here are some tips:

✦ Unless you tell it otherwise, when you ask it to search, Yahoo searches titles, URLs, and comments in its database and presents you with listings that contain all your keywords.

✦ Yahoo ignores the case of your keywords.

✦ By going to the Yahoo search page, you can tell Yahoo to do the following:

• Search only titles, URLs, or comments

• Pay attention to case

• Present matches with at least one keyword

• Present matches where your keywords only appear as substrings

• Limit the number of matches found

✦ Tell Yahoo to give you Internet sites or Yahoo categories that match your keywords.

If you have a Web site, you can ask Yahoo to add it to its index. See the Yahoo page for instructions.

Yahoo also has a Random button — click to see a randomly selected Web page.

Advanced Topics

This part talks about various Internet subjects that you don't need to think about right away. But once you get comfortable on the Net, you may want to consider these issues.

In this part...

✔ **Protecting your e-mail**

✔ **Building your own home page**

✔ **Chatting on IRC**

✔ **Playing in the MUDs**

E-Mail Security

As your e-mail message travels through the Internet, it passes through many different computers. Someone can intercept and read this message anywhere along the way without too much trouble. In this section, we tell you about some of the solutions people have proposed for improving e-mail security.

Key escrow

Key escrow is a new type of encryption technology in which a master key that can read all your messages is split into pieces. The pieces are stored for safekeeping at two different *escrow agents*—special organizations that promise not to give out your key information without proper authorization. This type of technology appeals to

✦ Those who run large organizations, who fear that an employee may abscond with the keys needed to decode vital data

✦ Representatives of law-enforcement and intelligence agencies, who need to read the messages of people considered a threat to society

Civil-liberties groups and many people on the Net are horrified by the idea of key escrow encryption, likening the concept to that of the police demanding a key to your home in case they ever need to search it.

The U.S. government's first attempt to push key escrow, the *Clipper chip,* has not caught on. A new, software-only, key escrow plan is in the works, and the European Union is working on a version of its own.

You can follow this debate on the newsgroup `talk.politics.crypto` on the Net.

Netscape Navigator 2.0

Netscape Navigator 2.0 is available from Netscape at `http://home.netscape.com/home/welcome.html` on the Web. It is a full Web browser that supports encrypted e-mail through a version of public key technology called *SSL.*

Netscape Navigator shows a key icon on the bottom left of the screen. If the key is depicted as broken, the connection is not secure.

Only the version of Netscape Navigator sold in North America offers full security. The export and free versions have been deliberately weakened to comply with U.S. export regulations. Even the fully secure version is believed to be less secure than PGP.

✦ By using Netscape Navigator 2.0, you obtain your public and secret keys from a central key vendor. The only company authorized so far is VeriSign, at `http://www.verisign.com`.

✦ VeriSign calls the keys "Internet Driver Licenses." They offer these licenses at the following four levels:

- *CLASS 1:* Low level of assurance used for secure e-mail and casual browsing. Noncommercial and evaluation versions are offered for free, with a VeriSign-supported commercial version for $6 per year.

- *CLASS 2:* Next level of assurance for a higher degree of trust and security. Used for access to advanced Web sites. Cost is $12 per year.

- *CLASS 3:* A higher level of assurance used for valued purchases and intercompany communications. Cost is $24 per year.

- *CLASS 4:* A maximum level of identity assurance for high-end financial transactions and trades. Pricing is application-specific.

✦ Netscape Navigator is very new and still being studied by cryptography experts, but the full-strength version may well offer easy-to-use encrypted e-mail with enough security for most users.

PGP

PGP, which stands for *P*retty *G*ood *P*rivacy, is a freeware encryption program with a strong following on the Internet. Here are some things you should know about this program:

✦ PGP is free only for noncommercial use.

✦ A commercial version of PGP is available in North America from Viacrypt, 9033 North 24th Avenue, Suite 7, Phoenix, AZ 85021; or send e-mail to `viacrypt@acm.org` on the Internet.

✦ Most experts consider PGP to be very secure if used correctly.

✦ The current version of PGP, Version 2.6.2, is harder to use than Netscape Navigator, but a more user-friendly version, 3.0, is expected to be released soon.

✦ PGP enables you to make your own public and secret key pairs.

✦ Public keys are distributed and certified via an informal network called "the web of trust," which is kind of like the letters of introduction popular in the pre-electronic era.

To learn more about PGP and how to get it, see Chapter 23 of *Internet E-Mail For Dummies* (IDG Books Worldwide, Inc.). You may also want to follow the newsgroup `alt.security.pgp`.

Public key cryptography

The solution to the Internet's security problem is a process called *public key cryptography*. Invented in the mid-1970s, this technology simplifies encrypted communication by enabling the general public to easily exchange *keys*, the short files of unique bits that let you scramble and unscramble your messages. Public key cryptology gives you two keys, one that you keep secret (your *private key*) and another that you can give to everyone (your *public key*). Here's how the concept works:

1. For two people (say, John and Arnold) to communicate by using encrypted e-mail, each must first have the other's public key in his computer.

2. John encodes messages to Arnold by using Arnold's public key.

3. Arnold decodes John's messages by using Arnold's secret key.

4. Arnold encodes his reply to John by using John's public key.

5. John decodes Arnold's reply by using John's secret key.

No one ever needs to give anyone else a secret code, yet everyone can communicate with privacy.

You can also use public key cryptography to sign your messages in a way that cannot be forged — unless, of course, someone somehow manages to discover your secret key. You encode your message with your own private key so that your public key is needed to decode it. This proves that you are the only one who could have sent this message. Both PGP and Netscape 2.0 support this feature.

Public key cryptography has been mired in hot political and legal controversy since it was invented. Many governments around the world, including the U.S. government, now wish that this technology had never been invented and are trying their best to control it. For example:

✦ Export of strong cryptographic software is illegal in the United States.

✦ The European Union is considering restrictions on cryptography.

✦ France and Russia have banned cryptography outright.

Two programs that use public key cryptography and are currently available on the Internet, PGP and Netscape Navigator 2.0, are described earlier in this part.

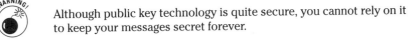

How secure is public key cryptography?

Subject to several big *ifs*, public key cryptography is quite secure.

✦ If the program you use is carefully written. Only careful scrutiny by cryptographic experts over an extended time, however, can determine just how carefully such a program is written. In the fall of 1995, for example, errors in the encryption code then used by Netscape enabled two graduate students, Ian Goldberg and David Wagner, to discover ways to break Netscape's code. Fortunately, those errors have now been fixed — and, we hope, this kind of public review will catch other errors quickly.

✦ If your key is long enough — *see* the following section.

✦ If no breakthroughs occur in the mathematical knowledge needed to crack public keys — progress to date has been slow, but steady.

Although public key technology is quite secure, you cannot rely on it to keep your messages secret forever.

How big should my key be?

Your public key is the product of two *prime numbers* — numbers that cannot be divided evenly by any other number. Your private key is the pair of prime numbers, each typically 75 to 150 digits long, used in making the public key.

Public key cryptography works because mathematicians have a difficult time figuring out the primes that produce the public key if the latter is big enough. As for what's big enough, RSA, the company that owns the patents on this type of public key cryptography, recommends that your public key be at least this long:

✦ For short-term security, 768 bits

✦ For medium-term security, 1,024 bits

✦ For long-term security, 2,048 bits

512-bit keys, the largest keys currently allowed for export, can be broken, albeit with considerable effort, by present-day technology.

Should I give out my credit card number over the Internet?

Several different views on this practice prevail.

One camp says that because so many other ways are available for crooks to steal credit card numbers, why worry about sending yours over the Net? Crooks can fish a discarded paper receipt out of a dumpster much more easily than they can intercept messages on the Net.

The other camp counters that computer use enables fraud to occur on a much more massive scale than have past methods. The best technology available, therefore, should be used to make cyberspace as safe as it can be, and everyone should insist on secure links before using the Internet for credit card and other financial transactions.

Web Home Pages

The hot, new thing on the Internet is having your own personal World Wide Web *home page* — a document with its own URL that can say anything you want it to. Some Internet providers, such as The World (`http://world.std.com`) and America Online's GNN, enable you to create and maintain a home page as part of your basic account, though often with some restrictions. Many other providers are willing to host your home page for a fee.

Why you would want your own home page

Reasons to have a Web page include the following:

✦ Advertising a business or hobby

✦ Publishing your ideas to the world

✦ Telling friends what's happening in your life (More than one prenatal ultrasound image file can be found out there.)

✦ Carving your initials on the Web for the fun of it

Building your page

Web pages are written in a computer language called *HTML*, which stands for *HyperText Markup Language*. A number of programs and word processor add-ons enable you to create HTML documents. To create a simple page, writing in HTML directly is not all that hard to do.

Most providers that support home pages offer HTML help files and sample pages that you can use as a starting point in creating your own page.

Most users of personal computers are familiar with the *What You See Is What You Get* (or *WYSIWYG*) concept of document preparation. In using WYSIWYG, authors are in complete control of how their document looks. HTML, on the other hand, is based on a very different model. Authors insert *tags* within their Webpage text that describe the function of various parts of their text, such as

✦ Headings

✦ Quotes

♦ Words requiring emphasis

♦ Addresses

♦ Lists

In particular, HTML ignores return characters and any extra spaces, except in text marked by the tag <PRE>.

The display program that reads the page — in this case, the *Web browser* — decides how these types of text appear on-screen. (*See* Part VI for more information about Web browsers.) The HTML concept is a throwback to 1970s text-preparation methods, but extensions are being added to HTML to give authors more control over the appearance of their pages. Netscape in particular is making strides in this area.

Most Web browsers enable you to read the HTML source text of any page you find interesting so that you can see how they do it.

An HTML document consists of text that contains *tags*. Tags, simply put, are *code strings* surrounded by an open angle brace (<) and a closed angle brace (>). These code strings tell a Web browser what to display. Tags, once activated, must be turned off by another tag with the same code but preceded by a slash character (/). The following are some commonly used HTML tags:

<A> ... </A>	This tag duo is an *anchor*. It indicates a *hypertext link*.
<ADDRESS> ... </ADDRESS>	These tags display the enclosed text in address style.
<BLOCKQUOTE> ... </BLOCKQUOTE>	These tags display the enclosed text as an indented block of text – typically used for a quotation from another source.
 	This tag starts a new line within a paragraph.
<H1> ... </H1>	These tags indicate a Level 1 heading, the biggest. Used mainly for page titles.
<H2> ... </H2>	These tags indicate a Level 2 heading, a medium size. Used for main subjects.
<H3> ... </H3>	These tags indicate a Level 3 heading, which is smaller in size. Used for secondary subjects.
<H4> ... </H4>	These tags indicate a Level 4 heading, which is smaller still. Used for tertiary subjects.
<H5> ... </H5>	These tags indicate a Level 5 heading, which is the next to smallest sized heading. Not good for much.

(continued)

`<H6> ... </H6>`	These tags indicate a Level 6 heading — very tiny. Used for fine print.
`<HR>`	Horizontal rule. This tag draws a line across the page.
`<LI>`	This tag indicates an item in an unnumbered list.
`<OL> ... </OL>`	These tags indicate an ordered list. Items in an ordered list are typically numbered.
`<UL> ... </UL>`	These tags indicate an unordered list. Items in an unordered list are typically bulleted.
`<P>`	This tag indicates the start of a new paragraph.
`<PRE> ... </PRE>`	These tags display the enclosed text "as is," using its native spacing and line breaks. A monospaced font is normally used, making <PRE> ideal for displaying tables or ASCII art — pictures drawn in characters.
`<EM> ... </EM>`	These tags emphasize the enclosed text, typically by displaying it with <u>underlining</u>.
`<STRONG> ... <STRONG>`	These tags display the enclosed text in a strong emphasis style — typically in **bold** type.
`<I> ... </I>`	These tags display the enclosed text in *italic* style.
`<B> ... </B>`	These tags display the enclosed text in **boldface** style.
`<TT> ... </TT>`	These tags display the enclosed text as typewriter text, which is typically shown in a `monospace font`.

Your Web page should be more effective if you follow these guidelines:

✦ Keep it simple. Focus on the essentials.

✦ Make yourself a sampler — an HTML document where you try out all the tags you want to use in your home page.

✦ Most Web users connect to the Net through a modem. Make loading large image files optional.

✦ Make sure that visitors have something to read while they wait for any graphics to appear on their screens.

✦ Content counts. Provide solid information, interesting artwork, entertaining stories, or something else to make a visit worthwhile.

✦ Check how your page looks on several different Web browsers. They can differ a lot!

✦ If you want people to visit your page, try to get it indexed at as many appropriate sites as you can (which is known as *Web weaving*).

Internet Relay Chat (IRC)

Internet Relay Chat (*IRC*) is an Internet service that enables you to communicate with people live, just as you would on the telephone — except that you type what you want to say and read the other person's reply on your computer screen. It's like CB radio, but on-screen. An entire Internet subculture has grown up around IRC.

IRC is available from most UNIX-based Internet providers.

AOL, CompuServe, The Microsoft Network, and Prodigy do not provide access to IRC. Instead, they provide their own live talk services:

✦ People Connection on AOL

✦ CB Simulator on CompuServe

Unfortunately, these services enable only subscribers on the same service to talk to each other. AOL, CompuServe, and MSN now support the Windows WinSock standard, however, which enables you to use Windows IRC client programs in conjunction with the provider's software.

Everything we said in Part III about people not always being who they say they are applies doubly to IRC. Be careful out there!

You can discover much more about IRC. Check out the newsgroup `alt.irc` or read the IRC FAQ at `rtfm.mit.edu`.

Starting IRC

The two main ways of using IRC are through the following:

✦ *Direct connection,* which is like a private conversation.

✦ *Channels,* which are like an ongoing conference call. After you join a channel, you can read what people are saying on-screen and then add your own comments just by typing them and pressing Enter.

If you are using a UNIX shell Internet provider that offers IRC, type **irc** at the UNIX prompt. If you have a SLIP or PPP account, ask your provider how to connect to IRC. If you have a direct link to the Internet, ask your system administrator if the link supports IRC.

Issuing IRC commands

You control what is happening during your chat session by typing IRC commands. All IRC commands start with the slash character (/). The most important command for you to know is

`/QUIT`

This command gets you out of IRC. The second most important command is

`/HELP`

which gives you an online summary of the various IRC commands. Other useful IRC commands are the following:

✦ `/ADMIN server` displays information about a server.

✦ `/AWAY` enables you to tell IRC that you will be away for a while. You don't need to leave such a message, but if you do, it is displayed to anyone who wants to talk to you.

✦ `/CLEAR` clears your screen.

✦ `/TIME` displays the date and time in case you can't take your eyes off the screen even for a moment.

✦ `/TOPIC whatwearetalkingabout` sets the topic message for the current channel.

✦ `/WHO channel` lists all the people on *channel*. If you type **/WHO ***, you see displayed the names of the people on the channel you are on.

If anyone ever tells you to type commands that you don't understand into IRC, *don't do it. Ever.* You can unwittingly give away control of your IRC program and your computer account to another person that way.

Remember: Everything you type while in IRC goes out to the Internet, *except* lines that start with a slash (/).

Choosing an IRC nickname

Everyone using IRC needs a *nickname.* This name can be the same as the user name in your e-mail address, although most people pick a different name. To choose a nickname, type the following:

`/NICK thenameyouwant`

Nicknames can be up to nine characters long.

Unlike e-mail addresses, nicknames can change from day to day. Whoever claims a nickname first on an IRC server gets to keep it as long as he or she is logged in. Nicknames are good only for a single session on IRC. If you chatted with someone named ElvisPres yesterday and then run into someone named ElvisPres today, there's no guarantee that it's the same person.

To find out more about the person behind a nickname, type the following:

`/WHOIS nickname`

The two main ways to learn someone's nickname are to see it on a channel or for another user to reveal it to you.

Holding a private conversation

To send a message to someone whose nickname you know, type the following:

`/MSG nickname whatyouwanttosay`

This method, however, becomes tiresome for more than one or two lines of text. You can instead start a longer conversation by typing the following:

`/QUERY nickname`

Now, whenever you type something that doesn't start with /, it appears on *nickname*'s screen, preceded by *your* nickname, immediately after you press Enter. Well, sometimes a lag occurs. . . .

Using IRC through channels

The most popular way to use IRC is through *channels.* Most channels have names that start with the # character. Numbered channels also exist (when you type a channel number, don't use the # character). You join a channel by typing the following:

`/JOIN #channelname`

After you join a channel, everything you type that doesn't start with a slash (/) appears on the screen of everyone in that channel, preceded by your nickname, after you press Enter. You leave a channel by typing the following:

`/LEAVE`

You can find out all the public and private channels by typing the following command:

`/LIST`

Before typing **/LIST**, type the following:

`/SET HOLD_MODE ON`

This phrase keeps the names from flying by so fast on-screen that you can't read them. Don't forget to set HOLD_MODE to OFF after you finish reading the list.

You can also limit the number of channels listed by typing the following:

```
/LIST -min 8
```

Only channels with at least eight people on them are listed when you type this phrase.

To get a list of channels and the nicknames of the people on those channels, type the following:

```
/NAMES
```

Pub means a public channel. You may see Prv, which means a private channel. The @ sign indicates a channel operator (*chanop*), who is in charge of managing the goings-on of the channel.

Good channels to know about include:

+ #hottub: Often a good meeting place

+ #irchelp: A place to ask questions about IRCs (Read the FAQ first.)

Starting your own channel

Each channel has its own channel operator, or *chanop,* who can control, to some extent, what happens on that channel. You can start your own channel and become its chanop by typing the following:

```
/JOIN #unusedchannelname
```

As with nicknames, whoever asks for a channel name first gets it. You can keep the name for as long as you are logged on as the chanop. You can let other people be chanops for your channel, but make sure that they are people you can trust. A channel exists as long as anyone is in it; when the last person leaves, the channel winks out of existence.

The following three types of channels are available in IRC:

+ **Public:** Everyone can see them, and everyone can join.

+ **Private:** Everyone can see them, but you can join them only by invitation.

+ **Secret:** Do not show up in the /LIST command, and you can join them only by invitation.

If you are on a private or secret channel, you can invite someone else to join by typing the following:

`/INVITE nickname`

If you get an invitation from someone on a private or secret channel and want to join, just type the following:

`/JOIN -INVITE`

Some people like to write computer programs that sit on IRC channels and make comments from time to time. These programs are called *bots,* short for *robots.* Just ignore them.

MUDs

MUD originally stood for *M*ultiple *U*ser *D*ungeon and was a way for Internet users to play an online version of the fantasy role-playing game *Dungeons and Dragons*™. MUDs, however, have evolved from those beginnings into a whole new way for people to interact electronically. The term MUD is now often said to stand for *Multiple User Dimension.*

If IRC is an Internet subculture, MUDs can be considered another solar system. Instead of a nickname, you need an identity — a fantasy role that you want to play in the MUD.

Many types of MUDs are out there, each with its own personality. You can find out more about MUDs by reading the `rec.games.mud.announce` newsgroup or by mailing a message consisting of the word `help` to the following Internet address:

`mudlist@glia.biostr.washington`

The `rec.games.mud` hierarchy encompasses groups for each major MUD type. Of course, it does offer a FAQ. One question found in the FAQ for this group is this: "Is MUDding a game, or an extension of real life with gamelike qualities?"

That should give you some idea of how devoted many MUDers are.

Internet Connections by Country

This appendix contains a long list of countries and lists Internet connection information for each one. The connection information is given in code letters.

The small table under "Code Letters Key" provides the key to the codes in the Internet "Connections by Country" list, along with what the codes mean.

Code Letters Key

Letter	Meaning
B	Full connection to BITNET network
b	Minimal connection to BITNET (five or fewer sites)
I	Connected to the Internet
U	Connected to UUCP dial-up network
u	Minimal connection to UUCP (five or fewer sites)
F	Connected to FIDONET dial-up network
f	Minimal connection to FIDONET (five or fewer sites)

All the networks listed here support e-mail. Only the Internet supports other services. Many small countries in the list still have no networks at all.

Connections by Country

Type of Connection	Country Code	Country
- - - -	AF	Afghanistan (Islamic Republic of)
- - - -	AL	Albania (Republic of)
- I - -	DZ	Algeria (People's Democratic Republic of)
- - - -	AS	American Samoa
- - - -	AD	Andorra (Principality of)
- - - f	AO	Angola (People's Republic of)
- - u -	AI	Anguilla
- I - -	AQ	Antarctica
- Iu -	AG	Antigua and Barbuda
BIUF	AR	Argentina (Argentine Republic)
- IU -	AM	Armenia
- - - f	AW	Aruba
- IUF	AU	Australia
BIUF	AT	Austria (Republic of)
b - U -	AZ	Azerbaijan
- - u -	BS	Bahamas (Commonwealth of the)

Type of Connection	Country Code	Country
b - - -	BH	Bahrain (State of)
- - U -	BD	Bangladesh (People's Republic of)
- lu -	BB	Barbados
bIUF	BY	Belarus
bIUF	BE	Belgium (Kingdom of)
- - U-	BZ	Belize
- - - -	BJ	Benin (People's Republic of)
- luf	BM	Bermuda
- - - -	BT	Bhutan (Kingdom of)
- - UF	BO	Bolivia (Republic of)
- - u -	BA	Bosnia-Herzegovina
- -uf	BW	Botswana (Republic of)
- - - -	BV	Bouvet Island
BIUF	BR	Brazil (Federative Republic of)
- - - -	IO	British Indian Ocean Territory
- - - -	BN	Brunei Darussalam
bIUF	BG	Bulgaria (Republic of)
- - U -	BF	Burkina Faso (formerly Upper Volta)
- - - -	BI	Burundi (Republic of)
- - - -	KH	Cambodia
- - Uf	CM	Cameroon (Republic of)
BIUF	CA	Canada
- - - -	CV	Cape Verde (Republic of)
- - - -	KY	Cayman Islands
- - - -	CF	Central African Republic
- - - -	TD	Chad (Republic of)
BIUF	CL	Chile (Republic of)
- luF	CN	China (People's Republic of)
- - - -	CX	Christmas Island (Indian Ocean)
- - - -	CC	Cocos (Keeling) Islands
blu -	CO	Colombia (Republic of)
- - - -	KM	Comoros (Islamic Federal Republic of the)
- - U -	CG	Congo (Republic of the)

(continued)

Type of Connection	Country Code	Country
- - u -	CK	Cook Islands
- luf	CR	Costa Rica (Republic of)
- - Uf	CI	Côte d'Ivoire (Republic of)
bluF	HR	Croatia
- - U -	CU	Cuba (Republic of)
bl - f	CY	Cyprus (Republic of)
blUF	CZ	Czech Republic
- lUF	DK	Denmark (Kingdom of)
- - - -	DJ	Djibouti (Republic of)
- - - -	DM	Dominica (Commonwealth of)
- luf	DO	Dominican Republic
- - - -	TP	East Timor
- lu -	EC	Ecuador (Republic of)
blU -	EG	Egypt (Arab Republic of)
- - u -	SV	El Salvador (Republic of)
- - - -	GQ	Equatorial Guinea (Republic of)
- - - f	ER	Eritrea
- lUF	EE	Estonia (Republic of)
- - - f	ET	Ethiopia (People's Democratic Republic of)
- - - -	FK	Falkland Islands (Malvinas)
- lu -	FO	Faroe Islands
- lu -	FJ	Fiji (Republic of)
BlUF	FI	Finland (Republic of)
blUF	FR	France (French Republic)
- - u -	GF	French Guiana
- - u -	PF	French Polynesia
- - - -	TF	French Southern Territories
- - - -	GA	Gabon (Gabonese Republic)
- - - f	GM	Gambia (Republic of the)
- - UF	GE	Georgia (Republic of)
BlUF	DE	Germany (Federal Republic of)
- - UF	GH	Ghana (Republic of)
- - - -	GI	Gibraltar

Type of Connection	Country Code	Country
bIUF	GR	Greece (Hellenic Republic)
- I - -	GL	Greenland
- - u -	GD	Grenada
- - uf	GP	Guadeloupe (French Department of)
- I - F	GU	Guam
- - uf	GT	Guatemala (Republic of)
- - u -	GN	Guinea (Republic of)
- - - -	GW	Guinea-Bissau (Republic of)
- - u -	GY	Guyana (Republic of)
- - u -	HT	Haiti (Republic of)
- - - -	HM	Heard and McDonald Islands
- I - -	HN	Honduras (Republic of)
BI - F	HK	Hong Kong
BIUF	HU	Hungary (Republic of)
- IUF	IS	Iceland (Republic of)
bIUF	IN	India (Republic of)
- IUF	ID	Indonesia (Republic of)
bI - -	IR	Iran (Islamic Republic of)
- - - -	IQ	Iraq (Republic of)
bIUF	IE	Ireland
BIUF	IL	Israel (State of)
BIUF	IT	Italy (Italian Republic)
- Iu -	JM	Jamaica
BIUF	JP	Japan
- - - f	JO	Jordan (Hashemite Kingdom of)
- IUF	KZ	Kazakhstan
- - UF	KE	Kenya (Republic of)
- - u -	KI	Kiribati (Republic of)
- - - -	KP	Korea (Democratic People's Republic of)
BIUF	KR	Korea (Republic of)
- I - -	KW	Kuwait (State of)
- - U-	KG	Kyrgyz Republic
- - - -	LA	Lao People's Democratic Republic
- IUF	LV	Latvia (Republic of)

(continued)

Type of Connection	Country Code	Country
- - U -	LB	Lebanon (Lebanese Republic)
- - u -	LS	Lesotho (Kingdom of)
- - - -	LR	Liberia (Republic of)
- - - -	LY	Libyan Arab Jamahiriya
- I - F	LI	Liechtenstein (Principality of)
- IUF	L	Lithuania
bIUF	LU	Luxembourg (Grand Duchy of)
- I - -	MO	Macau (Ao-me'n)
- Iu -	MK	Macedonia (Former Yugoslav Republic of)
- - U -	MG	Madagascar (Democratic Republic of)
- - - f	MW	Malawi (Republic of)
bIUF	MY	Malaysia
- - - -	MV	Maldives (Republic of)
- - U -	ML	Mali (Republic of)
- - uF	MT	Malta (Republic of)
- - u -	MH	Marshall Islands (Republic of the)
- - - -	MQ	Martinique (French Department of)
- - - -	MR	Mauritania (Islamic Republic of)
- - uf	MU	Mauritius
- - - -	YT	Mayotte
bIuF	MX	Mexico (United Mexican States)
- - - -	FM	Micronesia (Federated States of)
- IuF	MD	Moldova (Republic of)
- I - -	MC	Monaco (Principality of)
- - u -	MN	Mongolia
- - - -	MS	Montserrat
- - Uf	MA	Morocco (Kingdom of)
- Iuf	MZ	Mozambique (People's Republic of)
- - - -	MM	Myanmar (Union of)
- - U -	NA	Namibia (Republic of)
- - u -	NR	Nauru (Republic of)
- - u -	NP	Nepal (Kingdom of)
bIUF	NL	Netherlands (Kingdom of the)

Type of Connection	Country Code	Country
- - u -	AN	Netherlands Antilles
- - - -	NT	Neutral Zone (between Saudi Arabia and Iraq)
- - U -	NC	New Caledonia
- IUF	NZ	New Zealand
- lu -	NI	Nicaragua (Republic of)
- - U -	NE	Niger (Republic of the)
- - Uf	NG	Nigeria (Federal Republic of)
- - u -	NU	Niue
- - - -	NF	Norfolk Island
- - - -	MP	Northern Mariana Islands (Commonwealth of the)
bIUF	NO	Norway (Kingdom of)
- - - -	OM	Oman (Sultanate of)
- - U -	PK	Pakistan (Islamic Republic of)
- - - -	PW	Palau (Republic of)
- luF	PA	Panama (Republic of)
- - u -	PG	Papua, New Guinea
- - u -	PY	Paraguay (Republic of)
- luf	PE	Peru (Republic of)
- luF	PH	Philippines (Republic of the)
- - - -	PN	Pitcairn
BIUF	PL	Poland (Republic of)
bIUF	PT	Portugal (Portuguese Republic)
bIUF	PR	Puerto Rico
- - - -	QA	Qatar (State of)
- lu -	RE	Réunion (French Department of)
bluF	RO	Romania
bIUF	RU (SU is still in use.)	Russian Federation
- - - -	RW	Rwanda (Rwandese Republic)
- - - -	SH	Saint Helena
- - - -	KN	Saint Kitts and Nevis
- - u -	LC	Saint Lucia
- - - -	PM	Saint Pierre and Miquelon (French Department of)

(continued)

Type of Connection	Country Code	Country
- - u -	VC	Saint Vincent and the Grenadines
- - u -	WS	Samoa (Independent State of)
- - - -	SM	San Marino (Republic of)
- - - -	ST	Sao Tome and Principe (Democratic Republic of)
B - - -	SA	Saudi Arabia (Kingdom of)
- - Uf	SN	Senegal (Republic of)
- - u -	SC	Seychelles (Republic of)
- - - f	SL	Sierra Leone (Republic of)
bluF	SG	Singapore (Republic of)
- IUF	SK	Slovakia
- IUF	SI	Slovenia
- - u -	SB	Solomon Islands
- - - -	SO	Somalia (Somali Democratic Republic)
- IUF	ZA	South Africa (Republic of)
BIUF	ES	Spain (Kingdom of)
- IU -	LK	Sri Lanka (Democratic Socialist Republic of)
- - - -	SD	Sudan (Democratic Republic of the)
- - u -	SR	Suriname (Republic of)
- I - -	SJ	Svalbard and Jan Mayen Islands
- - u -	SZ	Swaziland (Kingdom of)
BIUF	SE	Sweden (Kingdom of)
BIUF	CH	Switzerland (Swiss Confederation)
- - - -	SY	Syria (Syrian Arab Republic)
BluF	TW	Taiwan, Province of China
- - uf	TJ	Tajikistan
- - f	TZ	Tanzania (United Republic of)
- IUF	TH	Thailand (Kingdom of)
- - u -	TG	Togo (Togolese Republic)
- - - -	TK	Tokelau
- - u -	TO	Tonga (Kingdom of)
- - U -	TT	Trinidad and Tobago (Republic of)
- Iuf	TN	Tunisia

Type of Connection	Country Code	Country
Bl - F	TR	Turkey (Republic of)
- - u -	TM	Turkmenistan
- - - -	TC	Turks and Caicos Islands
- - u -	TV	Tuvalu
- - - f	UG	Uganda (Republic of)
- IUF	UA	Ukraine
- I - -	AE	United Arab Emirates
blUF	UK (Also GB)	United Kingdom (United Kingdom of Great Britain and Northern Ireland)
BIUF	US	United States (United States of America)
- - - -	UM	United States Minor Outlying Islands
- IUF	UY	Uruguay (Eastern Republic of)
- IUF	UZ	Uzbekistan
- - u -	VU	Vanuatu (Republic of, formerly New Hebrides)
- - - -	VA	Vatican City State (Holy See)
- IUF	VE	Venezuela (Republic of)
- - U -	VN	Vietnam (Socialist Republic of)
- - - -	VG	Virgin Islands (British)
- I - f	VI	Virgin Islands (U.S.)
- - - -	WF	Wallis and Futuna Islands
- - - -	EH	Western Sahara
- - - -	YE	Yemen (Republic of)
- - uf	YU	Yugoslavia (Socialist Federal Republic of)
- - - -	ZR	Zaire (Republic of)
- I - f	ZM	Zambia (Republic of)
- Iuf	ZW	Zimbabwe (Republic of)

Usenet Newsgroups

There are over 10,000 Usenet newsgroups, with dozens of new groups (most of them short-lived) appearing every day. Rather than giving a list of every single group, worthless or not, this appendix lists some of the groups you might find interesting in each of the major hierarchies: comp, rec, misc, talk, soc, news, sci, and alt.

Computer Folk Talk about Computers (comp Newsgroups)

Traditionally, the largest set of newsgroups have been the computer-related ones under the comp hierarchy. It's not surprising: If you listen in on ham radio conversations, you realize that they're mostly about ham radio. So you may expect that when people used computers to create Usenet, they mostly talked about computers.

The comp groups can tend toward the esoteric and the technoid, but they're also a treasure trove when your computer acts up and you need advice from people who have seen it all before.

Many groups offer usable computer programs. The ones under comp.binaries are the places to look for free programs for PCs, Macs, and other personal computer systems.

Name	Discussion
comp.ai.neural-nets	All aspects of neural networks
comp.ai.philosophy	Philosophical aspects of artificial intelligence
comp.answers	Repository for periodic Usenet articles (moderated)
comp.binaries.mac	Encoded Macintosh programs in binary (moderated)
comp.binaries.ms-windows	Binary programs for Microsoft Windows (moderated)
comp.binaries.os2	Binaries for use under the OS/2 ABI (moderated)
comp.human-factors	Issues related to human-computer interaction (HCI)
comp.internet.library	Electronic libraries (moderated)
comp.multimedia	Interactive multimedia technologies of all kinds
comp.society	The impact of technology on society (moderated)
comp.society.privacy	Effects of technology on privacy (moderated)
comp.virus	Computer viruses and security (moderated)

None of the Above (misc Newsgroups)

Despite all the careful (well, sort of careful) arrangement of Usenet into meaningful hierarchies, some topics just didn't fit anywhere else; these topics ended up in misc, the miscellaneous hierarchy. Topics range from the totally staid to the hopelessly argumentative. The ultimate miscellaneous group is `misc.misc`, for discussions that don't fit *anywhere*.

Name	Discussion
misc.books.technical	Books about technical topics
misc.consumers	Consumer interests, product reviews, and so on
misc.education	The educational system
misc.entrepreneurs	Operating a business
misc.fitness	Physical fitness, exercise, and so on
misc.forsale	Short, tasteful postings about items for sale
misc.int-property	Intellectual property rights
misc.invest	Investments and the handling of money
misc.jobs.contract	Contract employment
misc.jobs.misc	Employment, workplaces, careers, and so on
misc.jobs.offered	Announcements of positions available

Time for a Break! (rec Newsgroups)

Even computer weenies like to have fun. (Stop laughing. It's true.) Usenet has lots of recreational groups for hobbies ranging from the strenuous, such as watching fish in an aquarium, to the totally relaxing — mountain climbing, for example. There are certainly a few here that you'll like.

Name	Discussion
rec.antiques	Antiques and vintage items
rec.arts.movies.reviews	Reviews of movies (moderated)
rec.arts.startrek.info	Information about the universe of "Star Trek" (moderated)
rec.arts.tv	The boob tube, its history, and past and current shows
rec.autos.driving	Driving automobiles
rec.birds	Bird-watching
rec.boats	Boating
rec.climbing	Climbing techniques, competition announcements, and so on
rec.crafts.brewing	The art of making beers and meads

(continued)

Name	Discussion
rec.crafts.textiles	Sewing, weaving, knitting, and other fiber arts
rec.food.recipes	Recipes for interesting food and drink (moderated)
rec.food.restaurants	Dining out
rec.gardens	Gardening methods and results
rec.railroad	For fans of real trains
rec.running	Running for enjoyment, sport, exercise, and so on
rec.skiing	Snow skiing
rec.sport.football.pro	American-style professional football
rec.travel	Traveling all over the world

Ask Dr. Science (sci Newsgroups)

A lot of Usenetters are in university or industrial research labs, so you'll encounter a number of scientists in the sci hierarchy (both professional and amateur). You'll also find many computer-science types, although (despite its name) this area isn't really a science.

In this hierarchy, you'll find pretty much any kind of pure or applied science you can think of, from archaeology to zoology and everything in between.

Name	Discussion
sci.aeronautics	The science of aeronautics and related technology (moderated)
sci.archaeology	The study of antiquities of the world
sci.astro	Astronomy discussions and information
sci.classics	The study of classical history, languages, art, and more
sci.crypt	Different methods of data encryption and decryption
sci.med	Medicine and its related products and regulations
sci.skeptic	Skeptics discuss pseudoscience
sci.space	Space, space programs, space-related research, and so on

Deep, Meaningful Discussions (soc Newsgroups)

Usenet is a sociable place, so naturally there's a great deal of socializing going on in the soc hierarchy. About half the soc groups are in soc.culture, where people discuss particular countries or ethnicities, and the other half are devoted to other sociable topics. You'll also find religious groups here, ranging all the way from fundamentalist Christianity to paganism to Buddhism.

Name	Discussion
soc.couples	For couples (compare with soc.singles)
soc.history	Things historical
soc.men	Issues related to men and their problems and relationships
soc.religion.unitarian-univ	A hangout for Unitarians, Universalists, and their noncreedal friends
soc.religion.quaker	A quiet, friendly group
soc.singles	For single people, their activities, and so on
soc.women	Issues related to women and their problems and relationships

Shooting the Breeze (talk Newsgroups)

A few topics provoke running arguments that never, *never* get resolved. Usenet puts these in the talk hierarchy, mostly to warn you to stay away. Most people find these groups to be argumentative and repetitious and populated mostly by students. However, *you* may not mind this, or you may feel differently — so take a look at any that seem interesting to you.

Name	Discussion
talk.abortion	All sorts of discussions and arguments about abortion
talk.answers	Repository for periodic Usenet articles (moderated)
talk.bizarre	The unusual, bizarre, curious, and often stupid
talk.rumors	For the posting of rumors

Usenet on Usenet (news Newsgroups)

What do people on Usenet like to talk about? Many like to discuss Usenet itself — endlessly. Here are some of the newsgroups in the `news` hierarchy that are worth reading.

Name	Discussion
`news.admin.net-abuse.announce`	Announcements about Usenet abuses (spams) that have been intercepted
`news.announce.newusers`	Information of interest to new Usenet readers
`news.answers`	A collection of the FAQs from most Usenet newsgroups in the `comp`, `rec`, `soc`, `sci`, `talk`, `misc`, and `news` hierarchies
`news.groups`	Discussions about forming new groups or rearranging existing ones
`news.lists`	Lists of useful information about newsgroups, mailing lists, and other Internet topics

Wild and Crazy Guys (alt Newsgroups)

So far, all the newsgroups we've discussed follow the Rules of Usenet. Then there are the newsgroups that don't — the `alt` newsgroups. To form a newsgroup in any of the preceding hierarchies, you have to write a serious proposal, sit through a 30-day discussion period, and pass a vote.

For those who have no patience for process, there are `alt` newsgroups. Any hacker can make one, and most do. Here are some of the tiny fraction of `alt` newsgroups that are worthwhile.

Name	Discussion
`alt.answers`	FAQs from `alt` newsgroups
`alt.config`	Discussions about forming `alt` newsgroups
`alt.dreams`	What do they mean?
`alt.flame`	Alternative, literate, pithy, succinct screaming
`alt.irc`	Information about IRC
`alt.paranormal`	Phenomena that are not scientifically explicable
`alt.save.the.earth`	Environmentalist causes
`alt.sex`	Postings of a prurient nature
`alt.tv.mash`	Nothing like a good comedy about war and dying

Name	Discussion
alt.tv.mst3k	Hey, you robots! Down in front!
alt.tv.muppets	Miss Piggy on the tube
alt.tv.prisoner	"The Prisoner" television series from years ago

Techie Talk

America Online (AOL): A commercial online service that provides many Internet services, including e-mail, Usenet newsgroups, Gopher, and access to the World Wide Web.

anonymous FTP: Using the FTP program to log on to another computer to copy files, even though you don't have an account on the other computer. When you log on, you enter *anonymous* as the username and your e-mail address as the password.

Archie: A system that helps you find files that are located anywhere on the Internet. After Archie helps you find the file, you can use FTP to get it.

archive: A single file containing a group of files that have been compressed and glommed together for efficient storage. You have to use a program like PKZIP, tar, or StuffIt to get the original files back out.

ARPANET: The original ancestor of the Internet, funded by the U.S. Department of Defense.

article: A message that someone sends to the newsgroup to be readable by everyone who enters the newsgroup.

baud: The number of electrical symbols per second that a modem sends down a phone line. Baud is often incorrectly confused with bps (bits per second). A 14,400 bps modem actually transmits at 2,400 baud.

BBS (bulletin board system): An electronic message system that allows you to read and post messages.

binary file: A file that contains information that does not consist only of text. For example, a binary file might contain an archive, a picture, sounds, a spreadsheet, or a word processing document that includes formatting codes in addition to characters.

bit: The smallest unit of measure for computer data. Bits can be *on* or *off* (symbolized by 1 or 0) and are used in various combinations to represent different kinds of information.

bitmap: Little dots put together to make a black-and-white picture.

BITNET: A network of mainframes that connects to the Internet.

bounce: To return as undeliverable. If you mail a message to a bad address, it bounces back to your mailbox.

bps (bits per second): A measurement used to describe how fast data is transmitted. Usually used to describe modem speed.

browser: A super-duper, all-singing, all-dancing program that lets you read information on the World Wide Web.

byte: A group of bits. Computer memory is usually measured in bytes.

channel: In IRC, a group of people chatting together. *See* Part XI.

chanop: In IRC, the *chan*nel *op*erator is in charge of keeping order in a channel. The chanop can throw out unruly visitors. *See* Part XI.

chat: To talk live to other network users from any and all parts of the world. To do this, you use Internet Relay Chat (IRC). America Online and CompuServe have similar services.

client: A computer that uses the services of another computer, or *server* (such as Usenet, Gopher, FTP, Archie, or the Web). If you dial into another system, your computer becomes a client of the system you dial into. (Unless you are using X Windows. Don't ask.)

client/server model: A division of labor between computers. Computers that provide a service other computers can use are known as *servers.* The users are *clients.*

communications program: A program you run on your personal computer that enables you to call up and communicate with other computers. Such programs make your computer pretend to be a terminal (that's why they are also known as *terminal programs* or *terminal emulators*).

CompuServe (CIS): A commercial online service that provides many Internet services, including e-mail, Usenet newsgroups, telnet, and access to the World Wide Web.

country code: The last part of a geographic address, which indicates in which country the host computer is, such as us for the U.S. For a complete list, *see* Appendix A.

digest: A compilation of the messages that have been posted to a mailing list over the last few days.

domain: Part of the official Internet-ese name of a computer on the Net.

domain name server (DNS): A computer on the Internet that translates between Internet domain names, such as xuxa.iecc.com, and Internet numerical addresses, such as 140.186.81.2. Sometimes just called *name server.*

download: To copy a file from a remote computer "down" to your computer.

dumb terminal: A screen and a keyboard and not much else. Dumb terminals connect to a mainframe computer.

elm: A full-screen UNIX mail reader. Another good one is Pine.

Eudora: A mail-handling program that runs on the Macintosh and under Windows.

FAQ (Frequently Asked Questions):
An article that answers questions that come up often in a newsgroup. FAQs are posted regularly, usually once a week or once a month. To read all the regularly posted FAQs for all newsgroups, read the newsgroup `news.answers` or FTP to `rtfm.mit.edu`.

FIDONET: A worldwide network of bulletin board systems (BBSs) with Internet e-mail access.

file-transfer protocol: A method of transferring files from one computer to another on a network or phone line. The most common dial-up protocols are Xmodem, Ymodem, Zmodem, and Kermit. The Internet has its own file-transfer protocol called FTP.

finger: A program that displays information about someone on the Net.

flame: To post angry, inflammatory, and insulting messages by e-mail or to Usenet newsgroups. Don't do it!

flame war: Two or more individuals engaged in a lot of flaming.

firewall: A computer that connects a local network to the Internet but, for security reasons, lets only certain kinds of messages in and out.

freenet: A free online system offering local communities information and limited access to the Internet.

F TP (File Transfer Protocol): A method of transferring files from one computer to the other over the Net. *See* Part VII.

FTP server: A computer on the Internet that stores files for transmission by FTP. *See* Part VII.

gateway: A computer that connects one network with another, where the two networks use different protocols.

GIF (Graphics Interchange Format): A type of graphics file originally defined by CompuServe and now found all over the Net.

Gopher: A system that lets you find information by using menus.

Gopherspace: The world of Gopher menus. As you move from menu to menu in Gopher, you are said to be sailing through Gopherspace.

gov: When these letters appear at the last part of an address (in `cu.nih.gov`, for example), it indicates that the host computer is run by some government body, probably the U.S. federal government.

HGopher: A cool Microsoft Windows program that helps you view Gopher information, including graphics right on-screen.

hierarchy: In Usenet, the major group to which a newsgroup belongs. The seven major hierarchies are `comp`, `rec`, `soc`, `sci`, `news`, `misc`, and `talk`. *See* Appendix B for listings.

home page: A Web page about a person or organization. *See* Part VI.

host: A computer on the Internet that you may be able to log in to by using telnet, get files from by using F TP, or otherwise make use of.

hostname: The name of a computer on the Internet. For example, the computer this glossary was last edited on is named `meg.tiac.net`.

HTML (Hypertext Markup Language): The language used to write pages for the World Wide Web. This language lets the text include codes that define fonts, layout, embedded graphics, and hypertext links. But don't worry, you don't have to know anything about it to use the World Wide Web.

HTTP (Hypertext Transfer Protocol): The way in which World Wide Web pages are transferred over the Net.

hypermedia: *See* hypertext, but think about all kinds of information, such as pictures and sound, not just text.

hypertext: A system of writing and displaying text that enables the text to be linked in multiple ways, be available at several levels of detail, and contain links to related documents. The World Wide Web uses both hypertext and hypermedia.

Internet: All the computers in the world talking to each other.

Internet Relay Chat (IRC): A system that enables Internet folks to talk to each other in real time (rather than after a delay, as with e-mail messages).

Internet Society: An organization dedicated to supporting the growth and evolution of the Internet. You can contact it at isoc@isoc.org.

INTERNIC: The Internet Network Information Center, a central repository of information about the Internet itself. To FTP information from INTERNIC, try ftp.internic.net. To see its Web pages, go to http://rs.internic.net/.

interrupt character: A key or combination of keys you can press to stop whatever's happening on your computer. Common interrupt characters are Esc, Ctrl+C, and Ctrl+D. Telnet's usual interrupt character is Ctrl+].

ISDN (Integrated Services Digital Network): A faster, digital phone service that operates at speeds of up to 128 kilobits per second.

Jughead: A program that helps you find information in Gopher by searching Gopher directories at a single host for information. Sort of like Veronica.

Kermit: A file-transfer system developed at Columbia University and available for a variety of computers, from PCs to mainframes.

kill file: A file that tells your newsreader which newsgroup articles you always want to skip.

link: Connection between one part of a hypertext document and another. (It can be a connection to another part of the same document or to another document.) On the World Wide Web, links appears as text or pictures that are highlighted. To follow a link, you select the highlighted material.

LISTSERV: A family of programs that automatically manages mailing lists, distributing messages posted to the list, adding and deleting members, and so on, sparing you the tedium of having to do it manually. The names of mailing lists maintained by LISTSERV usually end with -L.

lurk: To read a Usenet newsgroup or mailing list without posting any messages. Someone who lurks is a *lurker.*

Lynx: A character-based World Wide Web browser. No pictures, but fast.

MBone: The multicast backbone. A special subnetwork on the Internet that supports live video and other multimedia.

MacTCP: TCP/IP for the Macintosh. You can't put your Mac on the Internet without it. Comes with System 7.5.

mail server: A computer on the Internet that provides mail services.

mailing list: A special kind of e-mail address that remails all incoming mail to a list of *subscribers* to the mailing list. Each mailing list has a specific topic, so you subscribe to the ones that interest you. *See* Part V.

Majordomo: Like LISTSERV, a program that handles mailing lists. *See* Part V.

Microsoft Network, The (MSN): A commercial online service that provides many Internet services, including e-mail, Usenet newsgroups, and access to the World Wide Web. Only Windows 95 users can access MSN.

mil: When these letters appear as the last part of an address (the zone), it indicates that the host computer is run by some part of the U.S. military.

mirror: An FTP server that provides copies of the same files as another server. Some FTP servers are so popular that other servers have been set up to mirror them and spread out the FTP load to more than one site.

modem: A gizmo that lets your computer talk on the phone. Short for *mo*dulator/*dem*odulator.

moderated mailing list: A mailing list run by a moderator.

moderated newsgroup: A newsgroup run by a moderator.

moderator: Someone who looks at the messages posted to a mailing list or newsgroup before releasing them to the public. The moderator can nix messages that are stupid, redundant, or inappropriate (ones that are wildly off the topic or offensive, for example).

Mosaic: A Web browser that comes in Windows, Mac, and UNIX flavors. Versions of Mosaic have been written by several companies. *See* Part VI.

MUD (Multi-User Dungeon): This started as a Dungeons and Dragons type of game that many people can play at one time; now it's an Internet subculture. For information about joining a MUD, consult the newsgroup `rec.games.mud.announce`.

Netscape Navigator: A Web browser that comes in Windows, Mac, and UNIX flavors.

network: Computers that are connected together. Those in the same or nearby buildings are called *local area networks,* those that are farther away are called *wide area networks,* and when you interconnect networks all over the world, you get the Internet!

newbie: A newcomer to the Internet (variant: *clueless newbie*). Now that you've read this book, of course, you're not a newbie anymore!

news: A type of Usenet newsgroup that contains discussions about newsgroups themselves. Also used to refer to Usenet itself.

news server: A computer on the Net that receives Usenet newsgroups and holds them so you can read them.

newsgroup: A topic area in the Usenet news system.

newsreader: A program that lets you read and respond to the messages in Usenet newsgroups.

NIC (Network Information Center): Responsible for coordinating a set of networks so that the names, network numbers, and other technical details are consistent from one network to another. The address of the one for the U.S. part of the Internet is `rs.internic.net`.

nickname: In IRC, the name by which you identify yourself when chatting. *See* Part XI.

node: A computer on the Internet, also called a *host.*

packet: A chunk of information sent over a network. Each packet contains the address it's going to and the address from which it came.

page: A document, or hunk of information, available by way of the World Wide Web. Each page can contain text, graphics files, sound files, video clips — you name it.

parity: A simple system for checking for errors when data is transmitted from one computer to another. Just say none.

password: A secret code used to keep things private. Be sure to pick one that's not crackable, preferably two randomly chosen words separated by a number or special character. Never use a single word that is in a dictionary or any proper name.

PGP (Phil's Pretty Good Privacy): A program that lets you encrypt and sign your e-mail. Check in on `alt.security.pgp` for more information or point your Web browser at `http://www.mantis.co.uk/pgp/pgp.html/`.

Pine: A UNIX-based mail program based on elm. Pine is easy to use (for a UNIX program).

ping: A program that checks to see whether you can communicate with another computer on the Internet. It sends a short message to which the other computer automatically responds. If you can't *ping* another computer, you probably can't talk to it any other way, either.

PKZIP: A file-compression program that runs on PCs. PKZIP creates a *ZIP file* that contains compressed versions of one or more files. To restore these files to their former size and shape, you use PKUNZIP or WinZip.

POP (Post Office Protocol): A system by which a mail server on the Internet lets you pick up your mail and download it to your PC or Mac.

port number: On a networked computer, an identifying number assigned to each program that is chatting on the Internet. You hardly ever have to know these — the Internet programs work this stuff out among themselves.

posting: An article published on, or submitted to, a Usenet newsgroup or mailing list.

PPP (Point-to-Point Protocol): A scheme for connecting your computers to the Internet over a phone line. Like SLIP, only better.

Prodigy: A commercial online service that provides many Internet services, including e-mail, Usenet newsgroups, and the World Wide Web. For how to use Prodigy's Internet services, *see* Chapter 15 in *The Internet for Dummies,* 3rd Edition.

protocol: A system that two computers agree on to exchange information. A set of signals that mean "go ahead," "got it," "didn't get it, please re-send," and "all done."

router: A computer that connects two or more networks, including networks that use different types of cables and different communication speeds.

RTFM (Read The, uh, Fine Manual): A suggestion made by people who feel that you have wasted their time by asking a question you could have found the answer to by looking it up in an obvious place. A well-known and much-used FTP site named `rtfm.mit.edu` contains FAQs for all Usenet newsgroups.

serial port: The place on the back of your computer where you plug in your modem. Also called a *communications port* or *comm port.*

server: A computer that provides a

service to other computers (known as *clients*) on a network. For example, an Archie server lets people on the Internet use Archie.

shareware: Computer programs that are easily available for you to try with the understanding that, if you decide to keep the program, you will send the requested payment to the shareware provider specified in the program. This is an honor system. A great deal of good stuff is available, and people's voluntary compliance makes it viable.

SIMTEL: A computer that used to contain an amazing archive of programs for MS-DOS in addition to Macintosh and UNIX. It was run by the U.S. Army in New Mexico and was shut down in 1993. Fortunately, its files live on in mirror (duplicate) archives at oak.oakland.edu and wuarchive.wustl.edu.

SLIP (Serial Line Internet Protocol): A software scheme for connecting your computer to the Internet over a serial line. *See also* PPP.

smiley: A combination of special characters that portray emotions, like :-) or :-(Hundreds have been invented, but only a few are in active use. *See* Part III for a list.

SMTP (Simple Mail Transfer Protocol): The misnamed method by which Internet mail is delivered from one computer to another.

soc: A type of newsgroup that discusses social topics, covering subjects from soc.men to soc.religion.buddhist to soc.culture.canada.

socket: A logical "port" that a program uses to connect to another program running on another computer on the Internet. You might have an FTP pro-

gram using sockets for its FTP session, for example, while Eudora connects by way of another socket to get your mail.

spam: The act of posting inappropriate commercial messages to a large number of unrelated, uninterested Usenet newsgroups. It's antisocial and ineffective.

surfing the Net: Actually, we don't know what this phrase means, either. Maybe it means wandering around various Internet services, especially the World Wide Web, looking for interesting stuff.

TCP/IP: The system networks use to communicate with each other on the Internet. It stands for Transfer Control Protocol/Internet Protocol. *See* Part II of this book.

telnet: A program that lets you log in to other computers on the Net. *See* Part IX.

terminal: In the olden days, a terminal consisted of a screen, a keyboard, and a cable that connected it to a computer. These days, not many people use terminals because personal computers are so cheap. Of course, there are still lots of times when you want to connect to a big computer somewhere. If you have a personal computer, you can run a program that makes it *pretend* to be a brainless screen and keyboard — the program is called a *terminal emulator, terminal program,* or *communication program.*

text file: A file that contains only textual characters, with no special formatting characters, graphical information, sound clips, video, or what-have-you. Most computers, other than some IBM mainframes, store their text by using a system of codes named ASCII, so these are also known as *ASCII text files.*

thread: An article posted to a Usenet newsgroup, together with all the follow-up articles, the follow-ups to follow-ups, and so on.

Trumpet: A widely used newsreader program that runs on Windows.

UNIX: An operating system developed by AT&T.

upload: To put your stuff on somebody else's computer.

URL (Uniform Resource Locator): A standardized way of naming net-work resources, used for linking pages together on the World Wide Web.

Usenet: A system of thousands of newsgroups. You read the messages by using a *newsreader*.

uucp: An elderly and creaky mail system still used by a few UNIX systems. uucp stands for UNIX-to-UNIX copy.

uuencode/uudecode: Programs that encode files to make them suitable for sending as e-mail. Because e-mail messages must be text, not binary information, *uuencode* can disguise nontext files as text so you can include them in a mail message. When the message arrives, the recipient can run *uudecode* to turn it back into the original file.

Veronica: A program that helps find things in Gopherspace; a friend of Archie's.

viewer: A program used by Gopher, WAIS, or World Wide Web client programs to show you files that contain stuff other than text. For example, you might want viewers to display graphics files or play sound files.

VT100: The model number of a terminal made in the early 1980s by the Digital Equipment Corporation. Many computers on the Internet expect to talk to VT-100-type terminals, and many communication programs can pretend to be (emulate) VT-100 terminals.

WAIS (Wide Area Information Servers): Pronounced "ways," this system lets you search for files that contain the information you're looking for.

Web page: A document available on the World Wide Web. *See* Part VI.

WinGopher: A Windows program that lets you see Gopher pages.

WinSock: A standard way for Windows programs to work with TCP/IP. You use it if you directly connect your Windows PC to the Internet, either with a permanent connection or with a modem by using SLIP or PPP.

WWW (World Wide Web): A hypermedia system that lets you browse through lots of interesting information. According to some people, the central repository of humanity's information in the 21st century.

WinZip: A file-compression program that runs under Windows. It creates a ZIP file that contains compressed versions of one or more files. To restore these files to their former size and shape, you use PKUNZIP or WinZip.

Yahoo: A set of Web pages that provide a subject-oriented guide to the World Wide Web. Go to the URL http://www.yahoo.com/.

ZIP file: A file that has been compressed using PKZIP, WinZip, or a compatible program. To get at the files in a ZIP file, you usually need PKUNZIP or a compatible program.

zone: The last part of an Internet host name. If the zone is two letters long, it's the country code where the organization that owns the computer is located. If the zone is three letters long, it's a code indicating the type of organization that owns the computer.

Index

Symbols

<> (angle brackets), 169
* (asterisk), 130, 146
@ (at sign), 150, 174
\ (backslash), 106
^ (caret), 79, 80, 130
: (colon), 102
, (comma), 29
$ (dollar sign), 80, 130
" (double quotes), 158
= (equal sign), 61
! (exclamation point), 106
/ (forward slash), 61, 102, 106, 146, 169, 173
- (hyphen), 158
- (minus sign), 106, 140, 142, 158
. (period), 29, 80, 115, 130, 147
+ (plus sign), 79, 80, 81, 106, 140, 142, 158, 159
# (pound character), 173
? (question mark), 66, 106
> (right-arrow key), 47, 81–82, 133
[] (square brackets), 101, 158

A

<A> tag, 169
abbreviations, e-mail, 28
<ADDRESS> tag, 169
addresses, e-mail, 28–33. *See also* country codes; e-mail
   address books for, 49
   @ sign in, 28–29
   domains in, 30
   finding, 30, 34, 39, 49–51, 58, 161
   finger and, 151
   host names in, 28–31, 49, 50, 58
   host numbers in, 31
   for Internet For Dummies Central, 30
   IRC nicknames and, 172
   organization names in, 60–61
   postmasters, 55, 66
   registering, with Internet directory services, 49–51
   return, forging, 38
   used with mailing lists, 92
   X.400 standard and, 60–61
   zone names in, 30
Agent, 89
Anarchie, 134. *See also* Archie
anonymous FTP, 112, 123, 132, 195. *See also* FTP (File Transfer Protocol)

ANSI terminals, 154
AOL (America Online), 22, 195
   browsers, 100, 102–105, 122–124
   e-mail, 34–36, 52, 58
   FTP and, 122–124
   GNN (Global Network Navigator), 168
   Gopher and, 135–136
   IRC and, 171
   newsgroups access, 68–71, 73
   personalized home pages, 168
   talk and, 152
   Veronica and, 136
Appearance tab, 108
Applelink, 58
Archie, 127–134, 135, 195
archived files, 119, 120, 121, 195
ARP (Address Resolution Protocol), 24
ARPA, 6, 33
ARPANET, 33, 195
Article⇨Save, 87
asc command, 119
ASCII format, 114, 119
AT&T Mail, 58
attachments, e-mail, 49
ATZ installation string, 19

B

<B> tag, 170
back-up devices, recommendations for, 13
baud, 18, 19, 195
BCS (Boston Computer Society), 16, 17
Berkeley mail (UNIX systems), 36–38, 52
binary files, 195. *See also* uuencoded format
Binhex, 120
bin command, 119
bit, definition of, 196
BITNET, 33, 58, 178, 196
BIX, 58
<BLOCKQUOTE> tag, 169
bookmarks, 102
   in the AOL browser, 104–105
   in Gopher, 142
   in Lynx, 106
Bookmarks⇨Add, 109
Bookmarks⇨Go To Bookmarks, 109
Bookmarks menu, 109
Boston Computer Society (BCS), 16, 17
bots (robots), 38, 175
bottlenecks, during peak usage hours, 17
bps (bits per second), 18, 196

❏ YES!

Please keep me informed about IDG's World
of Computer Knowledge. Send me the latest
IDG Books catalog.

COMPUTER
BOOK SERIES
FROM IDG

NO POSTAGE
NECESSARY
IF MAILED
IN THE
UNITED STATES

BUSINESS REPLY MAIL

FIRST CLASS MAIL   PERMIT NO. 2605   FOSTER CITY, CALIFORNIA

IDG Books Worldwide
919 E Hillsdale Blvd, STE 400
Foster City, CA 94404-9691